GW01220374

RISK IN THE ROMAN WORLD

Modern risk studies have viewed the inhabitants of the ancient world as being both dominated by fate and exposed to fewer risks, but this very readable and groundbreaking new book challenges these views. It shows that the Romans inhabited a world full of danger and also that they not only understood uncertainty but employed a variety of ways to help affect future outcomes. The first section focuses on the range of cultural attitudes and traditional practices that served to help control risk, particularly among the non-elite population. The book also examines the increasingly sophisticated areas of expertise, such as the law, logistics and maritime loans, which served to limit uncertainty in a systematic manner. Religious expertise in the form of dream interpretation and oracles also developed new ways of dealing with the future, and the implicit biases of these sources can reveal much about ancient attitudes to risk.

JERRY TONER is a fellow, a tutor and the Director of Studies in Classics at Churchill College, Cambridge. He is a cultural historian whose work has a focus on history 'from below'. His book, *Popular Culture in Ancient Rome* (2009), analyses the life of the non-elite in Roman society. He has also written on Roman leisure and the Games, including *The Day Commodus Killed a Rhino: Understanding the Roman Games* (2014). He is interested in the use of classics to create imagery and stereotypes relating to subordinate groups, a theme explored in *Homer's Turk: How Classics Shaped Ideas of the East* (2013). Other areas of research interest include the sensory history of Rome and mental health in Antiquity. He came to the idea of risk from looking at how ordinary people developed coping strategies but also from his study of ancient disasters (*Roman Disasters*, 2013). There have been over thirty translations of his books into sixteen languages.

KEY THEMES IN ANCIENT HISTORY

EDITORS

P. A. Cartledge
Clare College, Cambridge
G. Woolf
UCLA

EMERITUS EDITOR

P. D. A. Garnsey
Jesus College, Cambridge

Key Themes in Ancient History aims to provide readable, informed and original studies of various basic topics, designed in the first instance for students and teachers of Classics and Ancient History, but also for those engaged in related disciplines. Each volume is devoted to a general theme in Greek, Roman, or where appropriate, Graeco-Roman history, or to some salient aspect or aspects of it. Besides indicating the state of current research in the relevant area, authors seek to show how the theme is significant for our own as well as ancient culture and society. It is hoped that these original, thematic volumes will encourage and stimulate promising new developments in teaching and research in ancient history.

Other books in the series

Death-Ritual and Social Structure in Classical Antiquity, by Ian Morris
978 0 521 37465 1 (hardback) 978 0 521 37611 2 (paperback)
Literacy and Orality in Ancient Greece, by Rosalind Thomas
978 0 521 37346 3 (hardback) 978 0 521 37742 3 (paperback)
Slavery and Society at Rome, by Keith Bradley
978 0 521 37287 9 (hardback) 978 0 521 37887 1 (paperback)
Law, Violence, and Community in Classical Athens, by David Cohen
978 0 521 38167 3 (hardback) 978 0 521 38837 5 (paperback)
Public Order in Ancient Rome, by Wilfried Nippel
978 0 521 38327 1 (hardback) 978 0 521 38749 1 (paperback)
Friendship in the Classical World, by David Konstan
978 0 521 45402 5 (hardback) 978 0 521 45998 3 (paperback)
Sport and Society in Ancient Greece, by Mark Golden
978 0 521 49698 8 (hardback) 978 0 521 49790 9 (paperback)
Food and Society in Classical Antiquity, by Peter Garnsey
978 0 521 64182 1 (hardback) 978 0 521 64588 1 (paperback)

Banking and Business in the Roman World, by Jean Andreau
978 0 521 38031 7 (hardback) 978 0 521 38932 7 (paperback)
Roman Law in Context (first edition), by David Johnston
978 0 521 63046 7 (hardback) 978 0 521 63961 3 (paperback)
Religions of the Ancient Greeks, by Simon Price
978 0 521 38201 4 (hardback) 978 0 521 38867 2 (paperback)
Christianity and Roman Society, by Gillian Clark
978 0 521 63310 9 (hardback) 978 0 521 63386 4 (paperback)
Trade in Classical Antiquity, by Neville Morley
978 0 521 63279 9 (hardback) 978 0 521 63416 8 (paperback)
Technology and Culture in Greek and Roman Antiquity, by Serafina Cuomo
978 0 521 81073 9 (hardback) 978 0 521 00903 4 (paperback)
Law and Crime in the Roman World, by Jill Harries
978 0 521 82820 8 (hardback) 978 0 521 53532 8 (paperback)
The Social History of Roman Art, by Peter Stewart
978 0 521 81632 8 (hardback) 978 0 52101659 9 (paperback)
Ancient Greek Political Thought in Practice, by Paul Cartledge
978 0 521 45455 1 (hardback) 978 0 521 45595 4 (paperback)
Asceticism in the Graeco-Roman World, by OP Richard Finn
978 0 521 86281 3 (hardback) 978 0 521 68154 4 (paperback)
Domestic Space and Social Organisation in Classical Antiquity, by Lisa C. Nevett
978 0 521 78336 1 (hardback) 978 0 521 78945 5 (paperback)
Money in Classical Antiquity, by Sitta von Reden
978 0 521 45337 0 (hardback) 978 0 521 45952 5 (paperback)
Geography in Classical Antiquity, by Daniela Dueck and Kai Brodersen
978 0 521 19788 5 (hardback) 978 0 521 12025 8 (paperback)
Space and Society in the Greek and Roman Worlds, by Michael Scott
978 1 107 00915 8 (hardback) 978 1 107 40150 1 (paperback)
Studying Gender in Classical Antiquity, by Lin Foxhall
978 0 521 55318 6 (hardback) 978 0 521 55739 9 (paperback)
The Ancient Jews from Alexander to Muhammad, by Seth Schwartz
978 1 107 04127 1 (hardback) 978 1 107 66929 1 (paperback)
Language and Society in the Greek and Roman Worlds, by James Clackson
978 0 521 19235 4 (hardback) 978 0 521 14066 9 (paperback)
The Ancient City, by Arjan Zuiderhoek
978 0 521 19835 6 (hardback) 978 0 521 16601 0 (paperback)
Science Writing in Greco-Roman Antiquity, by Liba Taub
978 0 521 11370 0 (hardback) 978 0 521 13063 9 (paperback)
Politics in the Roman Republic, by Henrik Mouritsen
978 1 07 03188 3 (hardback) 978 1 107 65133 3 (paperback)
Roman Political Thought, by Jed W. Atkins
978 11 07 10700 7 (hardback) 9781107514553 (paperback)
Empire and Political Cultures in the Roman World, by Emma Dench
978 0 521 81072 2 (hardback) 978 0 521 00901 0 (paperback)

Warfare in the Roman World, by A.D. Lee
978 1 107 01428 2 (hardback) 978 1 107 63828 0 (paperback)
Slaves and Slavery in Ancient Greece, by Sara Forsdyke
978 1 107 03234 7 (hardback) 978 1 107 65889 9 (paperback)
Roman Law in Context (second edition), by David Johnston
978 1 108 47630 0 (hardback) 978 1 108 70016 0 (paperback)

RISK IN THE ROMAN WORLD

JERRY TONER
Churchill College, Cambridge

CAMBRIDGE UNIVERSITY PRESS

CAMBRIDGE
UNIVERSITY PRESS

Shaftesbury Road, Cambridge CB2 8EA, United Kingdom

One Liberty Plaza, 20th Floor, New York, NY 10006, USA

477 Williamstown Road, Port Melbourne, VIC 3207, Australia

314–321, 3rd Floor, Plot 3, Splendor Forum, Jasola District Centre, New Delhi – 110025, India

103 Penang Road, #05-06/07, Visioncrest Commercial, Singapore 238467

Cambridge University Press is part of Cambridge University Press & Assessment, a department of the University of Cambridge.

We share the University's mission to contribute to society through the pursuit of education, learning and research at the highest international levels of excellence.

www.cambridge.org
Information on this title: www.cambridge.org/9781108481748

DOI: 10.1017/9781108592734

© Cambridge University Press & Assessment 2024

This publication is in copyright. Subject to statutory exception and to the provisions of relevant collective licensing agreements, no reproduction of any part may take place without the written permission of Cambridge University Press & Assessment.

First published 2024

A catalogue record for this publication is available from the British Library.

Library of Congress Cataloging-in-Publication Data
NAMES: Toner, J. P., author.
TITLE: Risk in the Roman world / Jerry Toner, Churchill College, Cambridge.
DESCRIPTION: Cambridge, United Kingdom ; New York, NY : Cambridge University Press, 2024. | SERIES: Key themes in ancient history | Includes bibliographical references and index.
IDENTIFIERS: LCCN 2023025906 (print) | LCCN 2023025907 (ebook) | ISBN 9781108481748 (hardback) | ISBN 9781108723213 (paperback) | ISBN 9781108592734 (epub)
SUBJECTS: LCSH: Risk–Rome. | Risk management–Rome. | Rome–Civilization.
CLASSIFICATION: LCC DG78 .T6575 2024 (print) | LCC DG78 (ebook) | DDC 937–dc23/eng/20230602
LC record available at https://lccn.loc.gov/2023025906
LC ebook record available at https://lccn.loc.gov/2023025907

ISBN 978-1-108-48174-8 Hardback
ISBN 978-1-108-72321-3 Paperback

Cambridge University Press & Assessment has no responsibility for the persistence or accuracy of URLs for external or third-party internet websites referred to in this publication and does not guarantee that any content on such websites is, or will remain, accurate or appropriate.

Contents

Acknowledgements		*page* viii
1	Risk and Uncertainty	1
2	A World Full of Risks	15
3	A Risk Culture	32
4	Risk Management	60
5	Moral Hazards: Constructing Risk	111
6	Conclusion	125
Further Reading		130
Bibliography		134
Index		144

Acknowledgements

I wrote this book against a backdrop of pandemic and war. Although planned some years previously, my ideas came together in a world where such events were permanent front-page news. I was fortunate enough to be largely cocooned from this reality by Churchill College, Cambridge, whose fellows have provided much helpful discussion about the nature of risk. The book aims to bring together and develop the various work I have done relating to aspects of risk in the Roman world. I am grateful to the editors of the Key Themes in Ancient History series, Paul Cartledge and Peter Garnsey when the book was commissioned, and now Greg Woolf, and to Michael Sharp at Cambridge University Press, for their patience, constructive criticism and enthusiasm for the project. As ever, I am particularly indebted to Peter for his long-standing support and friendship. Having children has made me alert to all kinds of risks I had never before considered, and I would like to thank Anne for helping me cope with them.

CHAPTER I

Risk and Uncertainty

A Risk Society

Risk defines modernity. We see it in almost every aspect of life, from disease to climate change, accidents to crime. Risks such as these pose a threat to our health, our safety, our finances and our mental health. The German sociologist Ulrich Beck has argued that Western civilisation is nothing other than a 'risk society', in which not only are our lives shaped by the calculation of probabilities but the number of risks has multiplied in line with innovations in technology.[1] Be it nuclear bombs or the threat of environmental catastrophe, Beck's world is packed full of the dangers created by scientific advances – except that they are no longer seen as advances. The old narrative of science as a force for good has been fundamentally weakened by innovations that threaten human existence itself. People have come to distrust the motives – as well as the statistics – of experts. As the Coronavirus pandemic showed clearly, experts disagree, often fundamentally, and, indeed, make errors in their predictions. Why should ordinary individuals believe and trust in experts when they can agree on neither the data nor its interpretation?

Paradoxically, therefore, greater scientific knowledge has resulted in greater general uncertainty. For Beck, this is a sign of a 'reflexive modernity', where respect for traditional sources of knowledge, such as scientists, has declined and left a void and a desperate feeling of anxiety and insecurity. Devoid of reliable and trustworthy sources of information, individuals are left to seek out their own knowledge about the nature of

---

[1] U. Beck, *Risikogesellschaft: Auf dem Weg in eine andere Moderne*, Frankfurt: Suhrkamp, 1986, translated as *Risk Society: Towards a New Modernity*, trans. M. Ritter, London: Sage, 1992. See also J. Franklin (ed.), *The Politics of Risk Society*, Maldon, MA: Polity, 1998, and S. Bennett (ed.), *Innovative Thinking in Risk, Crisis and Disaster Management*, Farnham: Gower, 2012. A good overview of the concept of a Risk Society and its place in wider risk studies can be found in D. Lupton, *Risk*, 2nd edition, Abingdon: Routledge, 2013.

the risks they face in their lives and have turned to all manner of 'alternative' experts in a search for reassurance, ranging from internet conspiracy theorists to the new certainties of various counter cultures. The globalised economy has generated an extraordinary array of life choices for the individual to make, but such choice has generated yet more fear. Taking the wrong course exposes individuals to risks and represents a failure on their part to understand the implications of their actions, a failure which only adds to their sense of anxiety. Not surprisingly, Beck argues, reflexive modernity has sought cover by taking control of all aspects of life and attempting to eliminate risk from ordinary life. Taking any form of unnecessary risk becomes an act of ignorance – an immoral refusal to understand the dangers implicit in a particular course of action.

Beck, however, sees risk as the product of modern capitalism. By definition, therefore, he denies that the concept existed in the pre-modern world. Risk represents what Beck calls 'a systematic way of dealing with hazards and insecurities induced and introduced by modernization itself', as opposed to 'older dangers', or what Giddens calls 'inclement nature'.[2] 'Human dramas', argues Beck, such as 'plagues, famines and natural disasters' and 'the looming power of gods and demons ... differ essentially from "risks" in my sense since they are not based on decisions, or more specifically, decisions that focus on techno-economic advantages and opportunities and accept hazards as simply the dark side of progress'.[3] Pre-industrial hazards were 'strokes of fate', no matter how large and devastating they were, and they were attributable to an outside 'other' and could be blamed on gods. Whereas modernity, in this view, has introduced a whole range of mega-risks, unlike anything seen before, in the pre-modern world 'danger' offered a sufficient range of vocabulary because an intuition existed of the possibility of future harm without there being much desire, need or ability to quantify it. Or as Joffe explains: 'The incalculable threats of pre-industrial society are turned into calculable risks in industrial society, in line with the modern project of promoting rational control in all spheres of life.'[4]

Beck's work has been highly influential in the field of risk studies and clearly has important implications for any proposed analysis of risk in the Roman world. And Beck is certainly not alone in seeing the ancients as

---

[2] Beck, *Risk Society*, p. 21; A. Giddens, *Modernity and Self-identity: Self and Society in the Late Modern Age*, Cambridge: Polity, 1991, p. 19.
[3] U. Beck, 'From industrial society to the Risk Society: questions of survival, social structure and ecological enlightenment', *Theory, Culture and Society*, 9 (1992), 97–123, p. 98.
[4] H. Joffe, *Risk and 'the Other'*, Cambridge: Cambridge University Press, 1999, p. 5.

passive victims of fate. The social theorist Tony Giddens also sees modernity as living 'after tradition', and 'is essentially to be in a world where life is no longer lived as fate'.[5] In this view, whatever disasters happened to humanity in the past were the work of an unseen divine or other supernatural power. They were events that were not, Beck concludes, 'politically charged'. We need think only of accusations that Nero deliberately caused the Great Fire of Rome in 64 CE to see that the reality in Antiquity was different. But, to be fair to Beck, as a social theorist, the ancient world has never been of much relevance to his work. Elsewhere he does appear to accept that risks have always been present, but he argues that the nature of modern risks is of a different order: the consequences of nuclear war are unfathomable and far greater than anything humanity has faced before.

As one writer has noted, 'risk is quite unique in the quantity and extent of research that draws upon it'.[6] But it is perhaps this denial of risk's existence in the pre-industrial world that explains why the subject has been of limited interest to scholars of Antiquity. The work that has been done is mostly on the Greek world and has been focused on peasant culture or on the use of divination to understand the future. Garnsey examined the frequency of food crises in Antiquity and how peasants and emperors responded to this risk. Gallant looked at the strategies adopted by peasant farmers in response to climatic variability and fluctuations in harvests. This included the cultivation of social relations to build up potential support networks. Grey adopted a similar approach towards the later empire. These books contain only brief discussions of what constitutes risk and how the concept might be applied to the ancient world, understandably preferring to focus on the specific practices they are examining. Grey's study of the effect of the eruption of Vesuvius contains a more detailed and useful discussion of the concept of risk in relation to that calamitous event.[7] Beard's article on Roman aleatory culture also contains useful observations on how Romans dealt with and even embraced risk.[8]

---

[5] A. Giddens in Franklin, *The Politics of Risk Society*, p. 26.
[6] A. Burgess, A. Alemanno and J. Zinn (eds.), *Routledge Handbook of Risk Studies*, London: Routledge, 2016, p. 1.
[7] P. Garnsey, *Famine and Food Supply in the Graeco-Roman World: Responses to Risk and Crisis*, Cambridge: Cambridge University Press, 1988; T. Gallant, *Risk and Survival in Ancient Greece: Reconstructing the Rural Domestic Economy*, Cambridge: Polity, 1991; C. Grey, *Constructing Communities in the Late Roman Countryside*, Cambridge: Cambridge University Press, 2011 and also 'Risk and vulnerability on the Campanian plain: the Vesuvius eruption of A.D. 472', *Journal of Interdisciplinary History*, 51 (2020), 1–37.
[8] M. Beard, 'Risk and the humanities: alea iacta est', in L. Skinns, M. Scott and T. Cox (eds), *Risk*, Cambridge: Cambridge University Press, 2011, pp. 85–108. I discuss this work further later.

Eidinow has published a popular book on the subject of luck, fate and fortune, which shows, in an accessible way, how ancient understandings and discussions concerning these concepts are still relevant to the modern world of risk. Beerden includes a more detailed discussion of the concept of risk in her work on divination in the ancient Greek world, although this follows a narrow, statistical approach, seeing the concept as a quantifiable uncertainty and therefore inapplicable to Antiquity. For her, divination was how the ancient Greeks dealt with their unquantifiable uncertainties. A similar approach is taken by Eidinow, who sees risk as 'quantified certainty' and therefore argues it cannot be applied to Antiquity.[9] Both these approaches provide excellent insight into how the practice of various forms of divination allowed the Greeks to try to manage the uncertainties in their life.

There is an increasing body of work dealing with the substantial threats that the Romans confronted. My own work looks at how the Romans thought about and dealt with disasters as a whole and the strategies they used to try to prevent them from happening, while there have been various studies that examined particular events, such as the Great Fire of 64 CE.[10] Scheidel and Harper have both provided comparative historical studies of plagues and pandemics and, in Scheidel's case, war.[11] Interest in the risks posed by climatic conditions and changes in Antiquity has also grown rapidly, with various attempts to interpret the historical data.[12] The Justinianic plague has seen substantial new research, including an increase in analysis of new forms of genetic evidence.[13] There is also an ongoing

---

[9] E. Eidinow, *Luck, Fate, and Fortune*, Oxford: Oxford University Press, 2011; K. Beerden, *Worlds Full of Signs: Ancient Greek Divination in Context*, Leiden: Brill, 2013; E. Eidinow, *Oracles, Curses, and Risk among the Ancient Greeks*, Oxford: Oxford University Press, 2007, pp. 196–203.

[10] J. Toner, *Roman Disasters*, Cambridge: Polity, 2013; V. M. Closs, *While Rome Burned: Fire, Leadership, and Urban Disaster in the Roman Cultural Imagination*, Ann Arbor: University of Michigan Press, 2020; J. J. Walsh, *The Great Fire of Rome: Life and Death in the Ancient City*, Baltimore, MD: Johns Hopkins University Press, 2019.

[11] W. Scheidel, *The Great Leveler: Violence and the History of Inequality from the Stone Age to the Twenty-First Century*, Princeton, NJ: Princeton University Press, 2017; K. Harper, *Plagues upon the Earth: Disease and the Course of Human History*, Princeton, NJ: Princeton University Press, 2021. On the late empire, see P. Sarris, 'Climate and disease', in E. Hermans (ed.), *A Companion to the Global Early Middle Ages*, Leeds: Arc Humanities Press, 2020, pp. 511–38.

[12] See F. L. Cheyette, 'The disappearance of the ancient landscape and the climate anomaly of the early Middle Ages: a question to be pursued', *Early Medieval Europe*, 16 (2008), 127–65; M. McCormick, 'Climates of history, histories of climate: from history to archaeoscience', *Journal of Interdisciplinary History*, 50 (2019), 3–30.

[13] See L. K. Little (ed.), *Plague and the End of Antiquity: The Pandemic of 541–750*, Cambridge: Cambridge University Press, 2007. On the genetic evidence, see L. K. Little, 'Plague historians in lab coats', *Past and Present*, 213 (2011), 267–90; M. H. Green, 'When numbers don't count: changing perspectives on the Justinianic plague', *Eidolon*, 18 (2019).

debate over the seriousness of the impact of both this plague and ancient climate change.[14]

There have also been many studies into various aspects of more specific risks that Romans faced. These have included demographic studies into life expectancy, given the significant threats of disease and malnourishment, and how these relate to the assumptions at work in Ulpian's Life Table of annuities. There have also been studies into a wide variety of ancient phenomena, ranging from military logistics, to legal aspects of uncertainty and maritime loans, all of which reveal something of how the Romans understood future danger. These are all examined in more detail in later chapters.

This book looks at how the Romans understood, thought about and dealt with risk. It sets out to challenge the views of Beck and Giddens in a number of ways. It argues that risk is a useful term to apply to Antiquity and that the Romans did not simply see themselves as passive in the face of fate. It argues that the Romans did display some understanding of risk and took a variety of steps to help manage it. And it argues that modernity's attitude to risk should not be seen as entirely unique. Pascal's 1654 discovery of probability represented a significant step forwards in the understanding of uncertainty. But it was a shift along a spectrum, not a sudden change from darkness to enlightenment, from total ignorance to knowledge.

Probability and Risk

Pascal's understanding of the stable relative frequencies of certain chance events meant that the future could be calculated and, for some, represents

---

[14] See K. Harper, *The Fate of Rome: Climate, Disease, and the End of an Empire*, Princeton, NJ: Princeton University Press, 2017. There have been several critical responses to this work, most notably J. Haldon et al., 'Plagues, climate change, and the end of an empire: a response to Kyle Harper's *The Fate of Rome* (1): Climate', *History Compass*, 16 (2018); J. Haldon et al., 'Plagues, climate change, and the end of an empire: a response to Kyle Harper's *The Fate of Rome* (2): plagues and a crisis of empire', *History Compass*, 16 (2018); J. Haldon et al., 'Plagues, climate change, and the end of an empire: a response to Kyle Harper's *The Fate of Rome* (3): disease, agency and collapse', *History Compass*, 16 (2018). Also, K. Sessa, 'The new environmental fall of Rome: a methodological consideration', *Journal of Late Antiquity*, 12 (2019), 211–55. Note also Harper's response to the critiques of him: K. Harper, 'Integrating the natural sciences and Roman history: challenges and prospects', *History Compass*, 16 (2018). On the impact of the plague, see also L. Mordechai and M. Eisenberg, 'Rejecting catastrophe: the case of the Justinianic plague', *Past & Present*, 244 (2019), 3–50; M. Meier, 'The "Justinianic plague": an "inconsequential pandemic"? A reply', *Medizinhistorisches Journal*, 55 (2020), 172–99; P. Sarris, 'New approaches to the Plague of Justinian', *Past and Present*, 254 (2022), 315–46.

'the underlying essence of risk'.[15] Once it was understood that there is a one-in-six chance of a dice throw producing a six, then this could be used to predict how later dice rolls would turn out. It is worth remembering that this is a model that will not necessarily correspond to the actual future. It may instead happen that the next three dice rolls all produce sixes, but the likelihood of this unusual occurrence could also now be calculated (as 6 × 6 × 6 = 1/216) and used to plot a normal distribution chart, known as a bell curve, which captures the likelihood of the various combinations of throws occurring. Pascal's discovery had significant implications for how uncertainty was seen, in that it could now be quantified, for decision-taking about what courses of action to take in the future, and indeed people's relationship with the future. Some aspects of the future were now mathematically knowable (which is not the same as knowable).

Interestingly, in the two centuries before Pascal's discovery, the notion of risk also emerged across Europe as a way to denote situations of potential damage to seaborne cargoes. We can interpret both as part of a societal shift towards a more calculating worldview, according to which people were trying to quantify unknowns and calculate the likelihood of certain outcomes and therefore make decisions about what was the best course of action to take. The term entered English during the 1660s from the French *risque*, itself derived from the Italian *riscare* (to run into danger), formulated from the medieval Latin *risicum*. As for the original etymology, as the *Oxford English Dictionary* notes, the origin of *risk* is 'much debated'. One theory is that the term risk comes from the Latin *resecare* (to cut off), from which the Spanish *risco*, cliff, derives, which obviously posed a threat to shipping; or that it comes from the Icelandic *ráðask* (meaning something like 'to decide to launch an attack'), a military term introduced into Latin following Norse attacks on the European continent; another possible source is the Arabic root *rizq*, meaning 'sustenance', 'income' or 'fortune', originally derived from the Persian *rozik*, 'daily bread'; or another is the Greek *rhiza*, meaning 'root' or *rhysis*, 'deliverance'. Whatever the ultimate source, it is clear that all these origins contain a sense of undertaking actions where there is the potential for both benefit and harm.

As for what the term risk has come to mean in the modern world, there is no simple consensus or accepted definition. In its simplest form, risk is

---

[15] Burgess, Alemanno and Zinn, *Routledge Handbook of Risk Studies*, p. 3. See also I. Hacking, *The Emergence of Probability: A Philosophical Study of Early Ideas about Probability, Induction and Statistical Inference*, 2nd edition, Cambridge: Cambridge University Press, 2006.

about the future. Since the future is unknowable, risk is also about uncertainty and the inability of humans to be sure of the consequences of their actions. It represents a lack of knowledge, since there can be no risk when there is certainty. Or, to put it another way, risk cannot exist in a predetermined world, a world of fate.[16] In a broad sense, therefore, we can see risk as relating to events where something is at stake and where the outcome is uncertain.[17] When dealing with probabilities, therefore, risk can be described as a neutral term, concerned merely with mathematically calculated losses and gains. In Frank Knight's classic book, *Risk, Uncertainty and Profit* (1921), risk was defined as an objective quantity that could be obtained by calculation according to the factors relevant to the outcome. By contrast, uncertainty was something more subjective and judgemental that could not be worked out mathematically.[18]

The Knight approach was later adopted in various areas of risk management and finance. In finance, risk was seen as representing volatility, which could be calculated based on the previous price behaviour of an asset. The more an asset's price moved the greater its volatility and risk. The capital asset pricing model took this further and argued that, for investors to attain higher returns, they had to accept higher risks.[19] One benefit of this approach is that, whereas the term risk tends to highlight the downside, volatility is a more neutral term that reflects the fact that risk can produce both good and bad results. The problem is that it is a predictive model that can estimate future outcomes based only on what has happened in the past. When events do not turn out as expected, the consequences can be dramatic. The collapse of the highly leveraged Long-Term Capital Management (LTCM) in 1998 and the 2008 Great Financial Crisis both showed that any calculation of risk in this way always includes a large element of qualitative assessment or reliance on past behaviour as an indicator of the future.

There are, then, limits to the calculation of risk based on probabilities. The calculation can be based only on *a priori* knowledge, as is the case with dice, where there is a limited range of possibilities, or it can represent a

---

[16] See S. O. Hansson, *The Ethics of Risk: Ethical Analysis in an Uncertain World*, Basingstoke: Palgrave Macmillan, 2013.
[17] For this definition, see E. A. Rosa, 'Metatheoretical foundations for post-normal risk', *Journal of Risk Research*, 1 (1998), 15–44, p. 28: risk is 'a situation or event where something of human value (including humans themselves) has been put at stake and where the outcome is uncertain'.
[18] F. H. Knight, *Risk, Uncertainty and Profit*, Boston, MA: Houghton Mifflin, 1921.
[19] For the classic paper, see H. M. Markowitz, 'Portfolio selection', *Journal of Finance*, 7 (1952), 77–91.

statistical probability based upon previous events, such as is done in insurance.[20] In real-life problems, the number of relevant factors is often so large as to mean that no *a priori* knowledge is usable. Also, real life tends to throw up unexpected or even unimagined outcomes. I sat on my Cambridge college's committee that examined the risk register and we never even considered the possibility of a pandemic. That is not a criticism but simply a statement that it is extremely difficult to plan for extreme events, let alone for what former US Secretary of Defense Donald Rumsfeld notoriously called 'unknown unknowns'. These unimagined risks have also been termed 'Black Swans', in reference to the discovery of such animals in Australia by Europeans to whom it had never occurred that such birds might have existed.[21] Whereas Knight's approach argued that uncertainty differed from risk because it was not reducible to numerically definite probabilities, Black Swan events showed that many situations threw up eventualities that had never even been imagined as possibilities. The financial calculations of the Nobel Prize–winning economists of LTCM generated a comforting sense of being in control until something unexpected blew them out of the water. In such a context, where there are so many variables and unknowns, risk calculations should not be seen as objective evaluations but more accurately as estimates, or 'judgements in the context of uncertainty'. They represent more of a subjective probability. Indeed, any risk that is fully measurable does not in reality represent an uncertainty, in that the future outcomes are known, and so there is no risk of any alternative scenario occurring. The boundary between risk and uncertainty has therefore become blurred at best.

Risk has always been a term used mostly of negative outcomes. It is therefore about danger and has become widely used to represent specific dangers themselves (as in, 'we face a number of risks'). Some people prefer to call these dangers 'hazards' as a way of differentiating from the act of risk calculation. So, a hazard can be seen as 'a set of circumstances which may cause harmful consequences', whereas risk is 'the likelihood of it doing so'.[22] This can be taken further, and risk can be calculated as the size of the hazard multiplied by exposure to it, where exposure means the extent to which the victim can be affected by the hazard.[23] The problem with this

---

[20] R. Boyne, *Risk*, London: Open University Press, 2003.
[21] P. Faulkner, A. Feduzi and J. Runde, 'Unknowns, Black Swans and the risk/uncertainty distinction', *Cambridge Journal of Economics*, 41 (2017), 1279–302.
[22] *Living with Risk: The British Medical Association Guide*, Chichester: Wiley, 1987, p. 13.
[23] A. Doyle and D. Ericson, *Uncertain Business: Risk, Insurance, and the Limits of Knowledge*, Toronto: Toronto University Press, 2004, pp. 4–5, define it as follows: 'risk is the frequency with which an

approach is that 'hazard' is a term that is rarely used as a noun in modern English, and its use attempts to force specific, technical meanings onto the term 'risk' when this has become widely used in a more general sense. Some might like to define risk as a scientific concept, but most calculations of risk involve the assessment of expectations of future behaviour based on knowledge and experience of the past, and knowledge and experience can be obtained by both formal and informal means. Tradition, custom, rules of thumb, estimates, judgements based on practice – all are ways that lay people can make risk assessments based on their own experience. Great bodies of scientific data may give a sense of objectivity compared with such common-sense calculations, but events such as the pandemic have highlighted the fact that such data are far from straightforwardly objective.[24]

One of the problems of trying to define 'risk' is that it serves only to limit what has become a broad term, used in a variety of ways:[25]

1. the chance or possibility of a usually negative event happening
2. danger or the cause of danger
3. the probability of an event happening
4. the size of the negative impact.

This variety of usage does not simply reflect a recent lack of precision, since the term has always been employed in a wide variety of ways since its introduction more than three centuries ago. The reality is that the term 'risk' is now used in all manner of technical and everyday contexts, but that frequency is itself a measure of how important a concept it has become in the modern world.

Despite this breadth, there are some shared implications in the use of the term. The first is that it suggests that the future can be changed – not necessarily controlled completely but influenced and to some degree altered by analysing the factors affecting possible outcomes and making judgements accordingly. As we have seen, some have argued that this represents a fundamental shift from the pre-modern past, in that the future is now manageable by humans rather than supernatural forces, a question to which I return. All risk concepts share this element in common: a belief

---

unwanted outcome is likely to occur and the severity of losses suffered when it does occur'; '[u]ncertainty is the lack of secure knowledge about an unwanted outcome'.

[24] See P. O'Malley, *Crime and Risk*, Los Angeles: Sage, 2010 and *Risk, Uncertainty and Government*, London: GlassHouse, 2004.

[25] See N. Luhmann, *Risk: A Sociological Theory*, trans. R. Barrett, New York: de Gruyter, 1993, pp. 1–31, 'The concept of risk'.

in the distinction between reality and possibility that means there is no room for fatalism.[26]

The second implication is that, since risk refers to the future, it in some sense exists only in the imagination. As we have noted, even Pascal's probabilities represent solely a model of what will actually happen when dice are rolled. If risk is a model for the future, then any more complicated calculation than dice-rolling is going to involve various assessments about what is acceptable or desirable as an outcome. This, by definition, involves a variety of value judgements. Risk, it therefore becomes clear, is a matter of perception and how it is perceived will contain a moral dimension.

Culture and Risk

While uncertainty can be seen as an 'objective feature of the universe', at least as far as human experience goes, risk is in the eye of the beholder.[27] Every society has a unique set of fears about the future that it prioritises over others. Different risk attitudes can be adopted by different societies to the same underlying uncertainty. The actions a society takes to alleviate these and the degree to which it treats them as acceptable depend on various cultural factors. In this context, it is evidently problematic to treat risk as an objective, technical concept. Instead, what constitutes a risk reflects a range of ideological, structural and social-psychological elements in a given social situation. Societies can in these ways be seen as revealing themselves by how they deal with dangers.[28] They have what can be described as specific risk cultures.

This approach was influenced by the work of the anthropologist Mary Douglas.[29] Douglas did not deny the reality of the underlying dangers: 'this argument is not about the reality of the dangers, but about how they are politicized'. She argued that there is always a moral dimension to risk-taking and that a failure to follow societal norms resulted in the victims themselves being blamed, especially in the modern world with regard to sexual behaviour and drug-taking. In this way, real dangers are used to give 'automatic, self-validating legitimacy to established law and order'.[30]

---

[26] O. Renn, 'Concepts of risk: a classification', in S. Krimsky and D. Golding (eds), *Social Theories of Risk*, Westport, CT: Praeger, 1992, pp. 53–79, p. 56.
[27] S. L. Savage, *The Flaw of Averages: Why We Underestimate Risk in the Face of Uncertainty*, Hoboken, NJ: John Wiley, 2009, p. 53.
[28] For the Roman case, see J. Toner, *Roman Disasters*, Cambridge: Polity, 2013.
[29] M. Douglas, 'Risk as a forensic resource: from "chance" to "danger"', *Daedalus*, 119 (1990), 1–16.
[30] M. Douglas, *Risk and Blame: Essays in Cultural Theory*, London: Routledge, 1992, p. 29.

This moral and political dimension also affected the allocation of resources within society towards certain types of risk reduction. All such allocation decisions were driven by whether society saw the risk as sufficiently threatening to make it worth the extra investment.[31] Risk, Douglas argues, has become a key idea for modern times because of its uses as a 'forensic resource' that has a meaning 'consistent with the political claims in vogue'. The term 'danger', she argues, 'does not have the aura of science or afford the pretension of a possible precise calculation'.[32]

It is possible to take this approach to understanding risk a stage further. Influenced by Foucault's theories of social discourse, risk perceptions are seen as the source of hazards themselves. The ways in which a society constructs risk represents a discourse, which concentrates on certain forms of uncertainty as being especially problematic. This narrative can harness and amplify risks to aid governmental control. Risk is in this view closely linked to power because it is often those in authority who have the ability to decide what constitutes a danger. The underlying hazard is itself seen as a cultural product that is invoked in a risk discourse to justify decisions regarding what constitutes risk, dangerous behaviour and the threatening individuals who engage in it. A risk has to be recognised as such, which will always involve an act of human perception, and such perceptions can be based on a variety of sources, including scientific data, everyday experience or religious beliefs. When different groups fail to agree on what constitutes a risk, it is not because they are interpreting the data differently, it is because different data matter to them.

From this viewpoint, risk does not exist in reality; rather, it represents a culturally embedded way of ordering reality that renders it into a calculable form.[33] It is a way of representing future events so that they can appear manageable. The significance of risk does not therefore lie with risk itself but with what it gets attached to. This anthropological approach sees all societies as developing reflexive mechanisms for the processing of perceived dangers, from fears that the sun will not rise again to natural disasters, potential catastrophes that are sought to be averted by various rituals. The concept of risk itself developed in a specific historical context, and

---

[31] Douglas and Wildavsky developed a grid system to characterize societal approaches to risk according to estimates of the degree of social stratification and social solidarity. See M. Douglas and A. Wildavsky, *Risk and Culture: An Essay on the Selection of Technical and Environmental Dangers*, Berkeley: University of California Press, 1982.
[32] Douglas, 'Risk as a forensic resource', pp. 3–4.
[33] M. Dean, 'Risk, calculable and incalculable', *Soziale Welt – Zeitschrift für Sozialwissenschaftliche Forschung und Praxis*, 49 (1998), 25–42, p. 25.

represented 'a new way of understanding the future and what harms or possibilities it might hold'.[34]

Early modern Europe, from 1500–1800 CE, was a place where the future was no longer seen as the realm of fate or fortune but one of calculable probabilities. The period, therefore, saw the development of a variety of ideas based on probabilistic reasoning and the possibility of acquiring more certain understanding of how future events would unfold and so guide decision making. It was an era where new kinds of political and economic organisation arose, such as central banks and insurance markets, which reflected this new approach to the future. The twentieth century saw an expansion of risk discourses into many other fields of expertise such as sciences, social sciences, medicine, and law, making it seem unique to what Beck and Giddens term 'advanced modernity'. Beck has little to say about the emergence of the concept of risk, but he does see risk calculation as symptomatic of modernity: 'induced and introduced by modernity itself'.[35] From a cultural standpoint, this represents a particular kind of cognitive activity focused on the assessment of potential outcomes rather than the discovery of anything real underneath. As Garland says: 'Risk begins where certain knowledge ends. Claims about risk are, literally, uncertain knowledge claims – impressionistic guesses, informed estimates, and probabilistic predictions about a future that cannot fully be known.'[36]

Risk is a multivalent modern term. Many studies of risk now adopt a broader, less realist approach to risk, seeing it as inseparable from the perspective of the viewer. Others retain a technical approach based on statistically quantifiable factors. As Cambridge University's Professor of the Public Understanding of Risk, David Spiegelhalter, notes, 'as it has gained in popularity, it has lost the sharp edges of definition'.[37] In practice, people tend to adopt whatever approach suits their aims. Actuaries, corporations and economists are more likely to use a statistical approach, whereas historians and anthropologists favour a more cultural definition.

---

[34] E. C. Nacol, *An Age of Risk: Politics and Economy in Early Modern Britain*, Princeton, NJ: Princeton University Press, 2016, p. 1.

[35] Beck, *Risk Society*, p. 21.

[36] D. Garland, 'The rise of risk', in A. Doyle and D. Ericson (eds), *Risk and Morality*, Toronto: University of Toronto Press, 2003, pp. 48–86, p. 52. See also J. C. Alexander and P. Smith, 'Social science and salvation: risk society as a mythic discourse', *Zeitschrift für Soziologie*, 25 (1996), 251–62.

[37] D. Spiegelhalter, 'Quantifying uncertainty', in Skinns, Scott and Cox, *Risk*, pp. 17–33.

Risk in Rome

How then am I defining 'risk' for the purposes of this book? I will definitely not be adopting the narrow technical approach, since this would mean that almost no risk analysis would be possible with regard to Rome. I adopt the popular and informal definition suggested by David Spiegelhalter, that risk is 'anything to do with situations when "bad" (or "good") things may, or may not happen'.[38] The crucial elements are simply that there is uncertainty and that the outcomes may be 'nice or nasty'. This last point is an important one. Most people instinctively see risk as a negative concept, focusing on the possible downside (indeed, it is noticeable that Spiegelhalter puts the 'good' in parentheses). But risk can also be seen as something that will generate significant variation in any outcome. Embracing risk can be a way for the individual to get richer, to improve his or her social status and generally move up in the world.[39] As I am interested in the ways in which risk was perceived and dealt with in the ancient world, I am alert to the discourses that were created around a very different set of risks than we would accept today, many of which related to religious ideas. Douglas was also right to see that risk involves a political blame game against those who engaged in what is seen as risky behaviour.

Perhaps more importantly, I restrict my approach to looking at areas where some element of calculation can be found in the Roman material, primarily relating to the period of the early empire. By this I do not mean numerical calculation of probabilities, since that did not exist, but areas such as law, religion, finance and seaborne trade, where the Romans also display various methods of probabilistic thinking, generally based upon experience and observation of the past, which show that they were concerned with trying to plan for an uncertain future. Lawyers, sailors and priests were the experts in ancient Rome. Ordinary Romans also had to make various assessments and judgements in the course of their everyday lives, and they relied more on the inherited wisdom of the past to reduce and control the risks they faced. These cultural tools were more communally calculated but still gave room for individual interpretation in their application.[40] These are all the focus of this book.

---

[38] Ibid.
[39] M. Blastland and D Spiegelhalter, *The Norm Chronicles: Stories and Numbers about Danger*, London: Profile, 2013, offers a very readable introduction to the use and abuse of statistics.
[40] On risk in daily life, see J. Tulloch and D. Lupton, *Risk and Everyday Life*, London: Sage, 2003.

This might seem a long way from the statistics generated by 'objective' risk studies. But what this introduction has tried to bring out is that a more cultural approach to risk moves away from this numerical approach, which sees risk as unique to the modern world. Looking at the various ways in which the Romans dealt with uncertainty serves to narrow the gap between us and them in that it shows us all trying to find ways to cope with the uncertainties we inevitably face in life. But it also widens the divide. If thinking about risk is always contingent upon historical and local contexts, and that knowledge is constantly contested and disputed, then we can expect that Roman ideas about uncertainty will be almost unrecognisable from our own. We must also remember that the 'Romans' were never a simple or static group. I am mainly concerned with arguing that various levels of understanding of risk can be found in the ancient sources, which relies heavily on the texts of the elite and evidence from the city of Rome itself, but I hope it will also become apparent that the inhabitants of the vast Roman empire represented a diverse set of peoples inhabiting many different circumstances. They all faced different types and degrees of risk and dealt with them in many different ways. Social status, in particular, dictated an individual's capacity to make decisions based on their own assessments. Slaves may have understood the risks of their situation but could not do much about them. Male members of the propertied class, by contrast, could consciously decide whether or not to invest in safe investments, such as land, or gamble on maritime trade.

CHAPTER 2

A World Full of Risks

Chapter 1 suggested that risk should be seen as an active concept, requiring an element of calculation designed to reduce and control future threats. It also argued that a spectrum existed between risk, at one end, and, at the other, a passively fatalist attitude to whatever the future held. Modern theorists, by contrast, have seen the development of the concept of risk as reflecting a profound shift away from a belief in the divine determination of human fate coupled with a decline in the power of organised religion.[1] According to Bernstein:

> The revolutionary idea that defines the boundary between modern times and the past is the mastery of risk: the notion that the future is more than a whim of the gods and that men and women are not passive before nature. Until human beings discovered a way across that boundary, the future was a mirror of the past or the murky domain of oracles and soothsayers who held a monopoly over knowledge of anticipated events.[2]

Modernity, it is also argued, has seen the introduction of new mega-risks, which far outstrip anything seen before. The aim of this chapter is to challenge these views in two ways. The first is to look at the range of concepts which did exist in Antiquity relating to uncertainty, which will show that the Romans were not simply fatalistic about what the future might hold or passive in the face of it. The second is to examine whether it is correct or reasonable to say that the ancients confronted less risk.

Ancient Thinking about Uncertainty

The ancients are often depicted as understanding themselves as being in the grip of inescapable fate and the will of the gods.[3] It has been argued

---
[1] G. M. Breakwell, *The Psychology of Risk*, Cambridge: Cambridge University Press, 2007, p. 1.
[2] P. L. Bernstein, *Against the Gods: The Remarkable Story of Risk*, New York: John Wiley, 1996, p. 1.
[3] See, for example, A. Giddens, *Runaway World: How Globalisation Is Reshaping Our Lives*, London: Profile, 1999, pp. 22–3.

that it was only once the world had moved away from such deterministic thinking that 'it became possible to see that the world might be regular and yet not subject to universal laws of nature. A space was cleared for chance.'[4] It is certainly right to say that deterministic views did exist in Antiquity. *Fatum* was what is spoken, that is to say, a prophetic declaration, generally concerning a bad end.[5] But coexisting with this idea were those concerning *fortuna*, which reflected the unpredictable element of the future and was personified in the goddess of that name who caused events to happen on a random basis.[6]

In his determinedly humanist and secular treatise *On Divination*, Cicero has his interlocutor, his brother Quintus, say: 'When the four knucklebones produce the Venus throw [one of each face] you may talk of accident. But suppose you made a hundred throws and the Venus throw appeared a hundred times. Could you call that accidental?'[7] For Quintus, a hundred consecutive Venus throws was so unlikely that there must have been some divine cause behind it. Yet it is also apparent that he understands a distinction between something happening by chance or at random and something being determined. He also understands that certain outcomes are so improbable as to be impossible without divine intervention. Cicero outlines his rejection of this view in the second book: 'Can there, then, be any foreknowledge of things for whose occurrence no reason exists? For we do not apply the words "chance", "luck", "accident", or "cause" except to an event which has so occurred or happened that it either might not have occurred at all, or might have occurred in any other way.'[8] Cicero should not, of course, be taken as representative of all Roman thinking. But both he and his brother show that a range of ideas existed that recognised the possibility of chance. Cicero also argues that certain unusual events cannot be seen as involving a divine hand: 'Nothing is so unpredictable as a throw of the dice, and yet every man who plays will at some time or other throw a Venus: now and then indeed two or three times in a row; are we going to be so feeble-minded to aver that this happened by the personal intervention of Venus rather than by pure luck?' In other words, determinism was likely to be discerned only in extreme situations.

Fortuna in itself was not a new, Roman notion, since the Greeks had their own concept of chance: *tyche*. Clearly, the ancients understood

---

[4] I. Hacking, *The Taming of Chance*, Cambridge: Cambridge University Press, 1990, p. 1.
[5] See Eidinow, *Luck, Fate, and Fortune*.
[6] See S. Sambursky, 'On the possible and probable in Ancient Greece', *Osiris*, 12 (1956), 35–48. See Lucretius, *On the Nature of Matter* 2.217 on randomness in the movement of atoms.
[7] Cicero, *On Divination* 1.13.   [8] Ibid. 2.6, after Loeb translation.

themselves as vulnerable to powerful divine forces, but vulnerable does not mean that there was no place left for any human agency. This took two main forms. The first was simply for humans to exercise free will and thereby seek to change the future by their actions. Cicero, in his discussion of fate, argues that to believe that the future is predetermined was an 'idle argument' because to accept that would lead to a life of complete inactivity.[9] If it is fated for you to recover from an illness, you will recover whether you call in a doctor or do not. At a more popular level, a fable tells how, after a shipwreck, one man kept calling on the goddess Athena for help while the others swam away. One of them shouted out to him, 'Move your hand to help Athena'. The moral of the fable spells out the message: 'we must devote some thought and action to our own cause besides praying to the gods'. Similarly, another fable emphasises that simply hoping things would turn out well was a poor strategy. Hence, in the fable of the hungry jackdaw, the bird sits on a fig tree waiting for the figs to ripen, but a passing fox says to him, 'You're a fool, my friend, to depend on hope. She'll lead you a merry chase, but she won't fill your stomach.'[10]

The second way for human agency to affect the future was to influence the decisions of the gods themselves. The passive resignation that a belief in fate suggests was not reflected in the usual understanding of the relationship between a worshipper and the gods. Characterised by the phrase '*do ut des*' (I give so that you might give), this reflected an asymmetrical patronage relationship with a client, who made offerings to a far greater power in the belief that this could influence that power into showing support and granting blessings. To be sure, the god would not always answer prayers and might still behave in a unfathomable manner, but at its core stood a belief that the future could be influenced, if not directed or controlled, by human action.

Human vulnerability to uncertainty also meant that the ancients went to great pains to try to make sense of the future by means of divination. It is possible to see this as reflecting a view of the future as being predetermined. It was human knowledge of what was going to happen that was profoundly uncertain. Just as the gods might be encouraged to help they were also generally believed to reveal what the future held in myriad different ways. The second-century CE Asia Minor Greek dream interpreter Artemidorus lists a variety of approaches, including the

---

[9] Cicero, *On Fate* 12.
[10] Aesop, *Fables* 30 and 126. The Fables can be found in the translation of L. W. Daly (ed.), *Aesop without Morals: The Famous Fables, and a Life of Aesop*, New York: T. Yoseloff, 1961.

interpretation of dreams, animal entrails, the flight of birds, the constellations, horoscopes, the face, the shape of the hand, dice, dishes, sieves and cheese.[11] There was, to use Eidinow's phrase, a thriving 'market in supernatural services' and the huge variety of forms that this took underscores how uncertain the future was seen to be.[12] This desire to find out what the future held did not reflect a passive acceptance of fate. It gave an opportunity to affect the future by offering gifts to the gods and thereby changing divine intentions and hence future outcomes. The fact that an entire pantheon of gods was believed to exist also meant that the idea of Romans being governed by a single fate is problematic, reflecting a Christian assumption that there is a single divine will. By contrast, the wide array of ancient gods, of varying powers and areas of interest, meant that the gods themselves could be played off against each other. By making offerings to alternative divine powers, the individual was able to affect, or at least have the possibility of affecting, future outcomes. Fate was itself manageable.

Cicero, in the second part of *On Divination*, argues against the possibility of knowing the future by means of the many ways in which it was widely believed that the gods communicated. Using signs such as 'the croak of a raven, the flight of an eagle, or the fall of a star' merely attempted to predict the future by means of studying random events that occur in the present. By contrast, he argues that it is possible to predict the future with some accuracy by means of reasoning and experience.[13] A doctor, for example, is able to anticipate the spread of a disease based upon his experience of seeing similar illnesses before. Cicero gives the further example of a general being able to anticipate the enemy's plans or the pilot of a ship forecasting the onset of bad weather, both of whom use their experience to assess what is likely to happen. But Cicero understands that such a process is not always accurate: even those who base their predictions on accurate reasoning are often mistaken. When a farmer, for example, sees an olive tree in bloom, he not unreasonably expects it will bear fruit, but occasionally this fails to happen. He makes his prediction on what has usually happened in the past and so can reasonably be

---

[11] Artemidorus, *The Interpretation of Dreams* 2.69, which can be found in translation in the Oxford World's Classics edition of P. Thonemann, translated by M. Hammond, 2020, or R. J. White, *The Interpretation of Dreams = Oneirocritica by Artemidorus*, Park Ridge, NJ: Noyes Press, 1975. On the difference between future-facing oneiromancy and psychoanalytic attempts to recover past trauma, see S. R. Price, 'The future of dreams: from Freud to Artemidorus', *Past & Present*, 113 (1986), 3–37.

[12] Eidinow, *Oracles, Curses, and Risk*, p. 6. [13] Cicero, *On Divination* 2.6.

expected to happen in the future. This is probabilistic thinking that Cicero ranks far more highly that any forecasts based upon such random events as dreams, portents and oracles.

The ancients clearly possessed a wide range of views about chance that reflected their view of the world as not simply being dominated by fate. While they did not develop any mathematical understanding of the principles of probability or its calculation, they did display some pragmatic awareness of the relative frequency of certain events.[14] Ehmig has showed how, in areas such as military supply and agriculture, data were regularly collected over extended periods and used as a basis for making decisions. Similarly, while Pascal developed his understanding of probability by thinking about card games, the ancients exhibited a similar interest in playing successfully at dice. The emperor Claudius is reported by Suetonius to have written a book on the subject.[15] We have no idea about the contents, but Suetonius describes the emperor as playing in a 'very learned' manner (*studiosissime*), which may suggest some understanding of frequency, likelihood or chance. But he also calls the book a description of the art (*arte*) of gambling, itself implying that this was not seen as a purely technical or numerical skill. Indeed, for Cicero, dice games and other games of chance, such as *micatio* and knucklebones, were all about 'audacity and luck', not 'reason and thought'.

This kind of preliminary thinking about probability is more easily discerned in dice oracles. For example, in the marketplaces of several towns in central Pisidia (an area in modern Turkey) there stood a tall rectangular marble pillar, on which were carved, in hexameter verse, the fifty-six replies of the gods to the fifty-six combinations that can be thrown with five knucklebones.[16] What is significant is that the oracles clearly understand that there is a limited number of permutations of five knucklebones. We know now that this can be calculated by a simple formula, but the numbers involved are sufficiently low that the total can easily be worked out in practice without it. It is tempting at this stage to ask why the Romans failed to notice 'the equi-proportionality property' of the fall of

---

[14] U. Ehmig, 'Antiker Umgang mit Wahrscheinlichem: einige Beobachtungen in den dokumentarischen Quellen', *Eirene*, 49 (2013), 90–116.
[15] Suetonius, *Claudius* 33 aleam studiosissime lusit, de cuius arte librum quoque emisit.
[16] The dice oracle and an alphabet oracle can be found in G. H. R. Horsley and S. Mitchell (eds), *The Inscriptions of Central Pisidia*, Bonn: Habelt, 2000, pp. 22–38 for the dice oracle, pp. 161–4 for the alphabet oracle. See also Graf, F., 'Rolling the dice for an answer', in S. I. Johnston and P. T. Struck (eds), *Mantikê: Studies in Ancient Divination*, Leiden: Brill, 2005, pp. 51–97.

the dice.[17] Part of the answer might be that the knucklebone does not fall equally, since two of the four sides fall much more often than the other two, but the Romans did also possess six-sided dice. Even if these were somewhat irregular, often being made from animal bone, they are unlikely to have produced highly irregular outcomes. To some extent, also, the answer could lie in a belief in the ability of divine power to affect the outcomes, meaning there was no possibility of any genuine randomness.[18] A story in Lucian gives a sense of this. A man who loved Praxiteles' statue of Venus (Aphrodite) would throw four knucklebones onto the table. If he threw well, particularly if he obtained the combination named after the goddess (when each dice landed on a different face), he praised the goddess. But if he threw badly, 'as usually happens', and got an unlucky combination, he was overcome by grief. There is a belief that the outcome is affected by the goddess, but there is also a recognition that it was usual for the throw not to land on the Venus throw; that some throws can be expected to happen more often than others. What is missing is any attempt to calibrate or quantify the variability.

When we do find attempts at calibration, they lack precision. Plutarch describes the attempt by the fourth-century Greek philosopher Xenocrates to calculate the number of syllables that could be produced by the various combinations of the letters of the Greek alphabet.[19] Xenocrates became head of the Academy at Athens in 339–8 BCE, a position which he held for twenty-five years, and according to Diogenes Laertius wrote treatises including *On Numbers* and *Theory of Numbers* as well as tracts on geometry, none of which survives. Plutarch says that Xenocrates calculated this as 'a myriad-and-twenty times a myriad-myriad'. It is possible to read this literally and interpret 'myriad' as meaning 10,000, in which case the answer is 1,002,000,000. Not only is this far too large a number, but the Greek word 'myriad' was also used to indicate a number too large to quantify, meaning that the philosopher was simply indicating that the answer was effectively innumerable or countless. Either way, it does reflect an awareness of the problem of calculating the number of possible permutations in a numerical fashion, which would be a prerequisite to calculating probabilities.

For a highly educated man such as Cicero, any attempt to predict the future based on random events was 'the invention of tricksters who were

---

[17] F. N. David, 'Dicing and gaming (a note on the history of probability)', *Biometrika*, 42 (1955), 1–15.
[18] Ibid. See also Hacking, *The Emergence of Probability*, pp. 2–10.
[19] Plutarch, *Convivial Questions* 733a.

interested in their own financial welfare or in following superstition and folly'. But Cicero was not the norm, even among the highly educated. Most people did perceive their futures as being to a greater or lesser extent influenced by divine powers, even though, as we have seen, that does not mean that they saw their outlook in fatalistic terms. We also find a deterministic worldview in the influential views of the fourth- to fifth-century Christian bishop Augustine, who came to believe that nothing happened by chance, that everything was controlled by the Will of God and that, however random events might appear, this reflected only a human inability to make sense of God's purpose.[20] This was not, however, the generally accepted view in the earlier, pre-Christian Roman world. Throughout the Classical period, ordinary people strove to understand their futures and to manage and influence them by means of various forms of divination. It was a way for them to cope with the significant uncertainties they faced.[21] Beerden comments that risk is the 'probabilistic thinking of modern Western man that, almost by default, he projects ... onto the ancient world'.[22] But the ancients did also display certain forms of probabilistic thinking and also sought to lessen uncertainty by trying to obtain perceived information from the supernatural concerning future events.

Risk is about imagining, understanding and managing the future and what it might bring. The notion of the future was conceptualised in very different ways by different sections of the population of the Roman empire, from the almost eternal claim to power made by the imperial authorities to the apocalyptic visions of a world free from Rome made by oppressed Jews and Christians.[23] In many ways, somewhat vague ideas such as Eternal Rome (*Roma aeterna*) reflected a lack of clarity about what was the long-term future of the empire. This was especially true in the work of Cicero, written during the civil wars of the late republic, when it was no longer even clear that Rome had a long-term future. For many writers, Rome's rise required explanation, something which also allowed for the possibility of analysing its prospects for continued success. Several historians, such as Polybius and Arrian, invoked a cyclical view of history to impart a lesson to their readers: that, if their empire was not to fall like

---

[20] *City of God*, 5.9.
[21] On fate, see H. S. Versnel, *Coping with the Gods: Wayward Readings in Greek Theology*, Leiden: Brill, 2011, pp. 218–20.
[22] Beerden, *Worlds Full of Signs*, p. 203. On risk, see pp. 196–203.
[23] On ancient concepts of the future, see J. J. Price and K. Berthelot (eds), *The Future of Rome: Roman, Greek, Jewish and Christian Visions*, Cambridge: Cambridge University Press, 2020.

so many had done before them, the Romans must work to maintain their pre-eminence, and even that might ultimately prove futile. That he had heeded the first part of this lesson was clearly one of the first emperor Augustus' messages in his proclamation of a new golden age. But Augustus had no intention of allowing for any futility in his enterprise. His imagery concerning his empire set out to construct the future as a form of unending present, in which the emperor's achievements in making Rome great again have the strength and authority to last in perpetuity, outdoing the empires that had been and gone before.

Such a confident view of Rome's future did not mean the Romans had a more linear understanding of time that allowed for the management of future events in practice. Shaw has looked at how the Romans had a variety of conceptions of the distant future by looking at activities ranging from state financing, strategic planning and public benefactions to long-term credit in private business transactions.[24] He argues that dominant Roman concepts of the future were largely short term and dependent on personal connections. Belief in the future relied on a network of trusted relationships to deliver the expected outcome. The understanding of a complex, more distant future was far less clear as a result. For example, when the emperor Marcus Aurelius faced a substantial fiscal shortfall following his campaigns in the north, he resorted to selling off his valuables from the imperial palace. What Marcus did not do was borrow against the future revenues of the state, because it never occurred to him, or indeed any emperor, to do that. The future, as a 'grander vision of a consistent space-time dimension', filled with 'things that are planned, known and solidly pictured', was lacking.[25]

Did Romans Face Less Risk?

Theorists such as Beck and Giddens see the late modern world as confronting new kinds of risk that sit on a different scale than those faced by pre-modern society. The threats posed by nuclear war and climate change mean that risk itself is perceived differently, in that it is seen as affecting everyone in an existential, life-or-death struggle for the survival of the entire species. Risk has become universal, threatening all of humanity. It is also argued that these modern mega-risks differ because of their invisibility.

---

[24] B. D. Shaw, 'Did the Romans have a future?', *Journal of Roman Studies*, 109 (2019), 1–26.
[25] Ibid., p. 6.

We know nuclear bombs exist but only in an abstract sense, in that most people have never seen one, and radiation is impossible for the lay person to detect. Similarly, we can see some elements of climate change taking place already, but we cannot see the carbon in the air, and many of the real dangers lie in the statistical modelling of future outcomes as mediated by experts.

At first glance, there is something to be said for these arguments. The ancient world did not possess the kind of technology to generate nuclear Armageddon, and the Romans were largely concerned with threats that they knew existed or had experienced before. But there are a number of challenges to these views. First is the question of the size of the risk posed by modern threats in comparison to those experienced in the ancient world. The Earth Institute at Columbia University has estimated the 'mortality cost of carbon' as causing up to 83 million deaths by 2100. This number excludes those who might die from other effects such as rising sea levels, increased storm activity and crop failures. This is an estimate based on a severe rise in global temperatures of 4.1 degrees Celsius. On the current level of eight billion, that represents approximately 1 per cent of the global population. Obviously there will be a variety of other severe but non-lethal side effects from a rise in global temperature of this magnitude, but as a mortality rate, disastrous as this will be, it is not out of kilter with the ancient world's. Comparative evidence suggests that an individual born in Antiquity had a life expectancy at birth of approximately twenty-five years, about one-third of that in the Western world today. Poor sanitation, lack of basic hygiene and limited medical knowledge all combined to make early death widespread, with infants in particular being affected. About a third of all babies died in their first year of life. About half of all children were dead before their fifth birthday. Make it to ten and you could reasonably expect to live to fifty. But not many made it to what we would think of as retirement age. Grandparents were a rarity, missing parents and orphans commonplace.

The consequences of nuclear war are hard to estimate but a poll of experts at the Global Catastrophic Risk Conference in Oxford (17–20 July 2008) estimated the probability of complete human extinction by nuclear weapons at 1 per cent within the century, the probability of one billion dead at 10 per cent and the probability of one million dead at 30 per cent. These numbers are not based on any probabilistic modelling and are no more than educated guesses. They also do not account for the many other terrible consequences of a global nuclear war. But as a percentage of global population, one billion would represent 12.5 per cent.[26] An average life expectancy of twenty-five years means that about 4 per cent of all Romans were dying each year, primarily as a result of the basic factors mentioned earlier. In other words, every three years the equivalent number was dying as are predicted for a serious nuclear conflict.

A nuclear war would affect the main adversaries the worst. A 1979 report for the US Senate estimated casualties under a full-scale nuclear exchange between the USA and the then Soviet Union would cause American deaths of 35 to 77 per cent of the population, and Soviet deaths of 20 to 40 per cent.[27] These are terrifying statistics but it is worth comparing this kind of impact with the worst of the plagues that afflicted the ancient world. In the Great Plague, most likely the first outbreak of bubonic plague, which started in 541 CE, the contemporary Greek author Procopius recounts that 'the whole human race came near to being annihilated'.[28] He claims that the death toll in Constantinople reached a peak of 10,000 a day for three months. John of Ephesus recounts that during the plague, '[s]ometimes five, seven, twelve and up to sixteen thousand persons among them were removed in a day'.[29] 'Thus', we are told, 'the poor vanished, though a small number of them survived'. Of course, ancient writers had no access to reliable information regarding the number of casualties because no such information existed. They relied on estimates, numbers given by other writers for similar disasters and hearsay. Terrible events, such as plague, caused death on a scale that made accuracy even more difficult. Even if we take a lower figure than did Procopius of 3,000 per day, we come to a total mortality figure of about 300,000, which looks much too high, given that the likely population of Constantinople at that time was not much more than that. The impact was evidently substantial and affected all classes: 'all one could see now was a great and violent blow that suddenly struck ordinary people and nobles alike'. The later bubonic plague in the fourteenth century is estimated to have killed about one-third of the population of Europe. This may have been a more serious plague, but it suggests that estimates of 15–25 per cent

---

[26] A. Sandberg and N. Bostrom, *Global Catastrophic Risks Survey*, Technical Report #2008-1, Future of Humanity Institute, Oxford University.
[27] L. S. Johns et al., *The Effects of Nuclear War*, Washington, DC: Library of Congress, 1979.
[28] Procopius, *Wars* 2.22.1 and 2.23.1. For a comparative historical study of plagues, pandemics and war, see W. Scheidel, *The Great Leveler: Violence and the History of Inequality from the Stone Age to the Twenty-First Century*, Princeton, NJ.: Princeton University Press, 2017.
[29] John of Ephesus, *4th Account* in *The Chronicle of Zuqnīn*, parts III and IV: AD 488–775, trans. A. Harrak, Toronto: Pontifical Institute of Mediaeval Studies, 1999.

mortality for the Great Plague of 541 would not be unreasonable. This is broadly comparable with the death toll of a major nuclear conflict. Nor was this the only serious plague to hit Antiquity. Earlier plagues, such as the Antonine Plague of the late second century CE, possibly an outbreak of smallpox, probably had a lesser impact but, according to some estimates, killed about 10 per cent of the population of the Roman empire.

There are many problems with this comparison. The data are unreliable, the additional side effects are even harder to quantify and the range of possible outcomes is huge. The main point, however, is that, horrifying as the risk of nuclear war might be, in terms of estimated population loss it is not of a completely different order than was faced in Antiquity. It is also worth noting that the ancients had no idea about the cause of these plagues. They knew nothing about the causes of disease, mostly experiencing the plague as a sudden and invisible catastrophe sent from the heavens as a punishment for human wrongdoing. Plague for them was as invisible as nuclear radiation.

Plague was also just one of the many significant risks to their life and limb that the Romans faced. Tacitus, for example, records that 20,000 were maimed or killed when the amphitheatre at Fidenae, about five miles north of Rome, collapsed in 27 CE.[30] The sixth-century CE historian John of Ephesus states in his account of the siege of Amida that 80,000 corpses were found after its fall. John also gives a figure of 250,000 deaths after an earthquake in Antioch in 526 CE. The unreliability of these data is highlighted by the fact that another historian, Evagrius, gives a number of 60,000 for a later earthquake in the same city.[31] This is not to single out John of Ephesus for particular criticism. It is a problem with many ancient accounts of disaster that they often wish it to appear in the worst possible light in order to justify their own recording of it. Again, the point is not to treat these numbers as accurate but to emphasise that even lower estimates produce levels of casualties that are almost never experienced in modernity.

The Roman world was full of insecurity, and its inhabitants were systematically exposed to a variety of routine dangers in both individual and communal ways. The very routineness of such dangers meant that they were largely ignored. Physical insecurities included hunger, cold, physical weakness resulting from disease or poor nutrition and death caused by disease. All of these were exacerbated by the impact of war and violence. Food supply depended upon the volatile Mediterranean

---

[30] Tacitus, *Annals* 4.63. On disasters, see Toner, *Roman Disasters*.
[31] Evagrius, *Church History* 6.8.

climate, which resulted in significant variation in annual harvests. The Romans relied on fire for cooking, heating and light. Many other crafts depended on fire to enable them to pursue their trades: baking, glass-making, metalwork and felt-making all needed fire to function. In a densely inhabited city such as Rome, where timber acted as the primary building material, the very fabric of the infrastructure left it permanently at risk of a disastrous conflagration. Tacitus records that the Great Fire of 64 CE destroyed eleven of the city's fourteen districts. He gives no figure for the number of casualties, but it was likely to have been high given the size of the fire and the speed with which it spread. Ancient society's ability to reduce the impact of these events was diminished by the disinterest and limited capabilities of the Roman state in what were generally seen as individual concerns. The Romans had no choice but to accept the imminence of death, sickness and injury as a normal part of everyday life in a way that the inhabitants of modernity do not.

One area of substantial risk was travel, as the Romans knew only too well. Thinking about the sea brought to mind great uncertainties. The replies of Secundus, the Silent Philosopher, to the question 'what is a boat?' included 'fate bound up in a package', 'uncertain safety', and 'death in prospect'.[32] The stress that being caught in a storm could create was substantial, as is revealed in some ancient jokes. When a coward was asked, 'what ships are safer, warships or merchant ships?' his reply was: 'Docked ships'.[33] Shipwreck was a very real risk in the ancient world: hundreds of ancient wrecks have been detected in the Mediterranean, and there are doubtless many more that remain undiscovered. Most on board will have died from drowning, suffering what Achilles Tatius calls, in his novel *Leucippe and Clitophon*, 'the prolonged terror of a slow sea death, which kills you a thousand times before you die', a long drawn-out process where the fear is 'infinitely multiplied by the ocean's endless vista'. The lucky ones were killed quickly by being dashed on the rocks or impaled on the points of shattering planks 'like speared fish'.[34]

Health risks abounded and rich and poor alike experienced high levels of morbidity. Young children in particular will have suffered high levels of sickness. While death from illness was doubtless a significant background concern for all ages, it was the risk of falling ill and being unable to earn a

---

[32] See W. Hansen (ed.), *Anthology of Ancient Greek Popular Literature*, Bloomington: Indiana University Press, 1998, p. 73.
[33] *Laughter-Lover* 206; on the dangers of sea travel, see also 30, 81 and *Acts* 27:14–44.
[34] *Leucippe and Clitophon* 3.2–5 in B. P. Reardon (ed.), *Collected Ancient Greek Novels*, Berkeley: University of California Press, 1989.

living that posed a more everyday concern for most non-elite adults. High-density urban population levels combined with poor sanitation will have exacerbated morbidity levels. Exposure to persistently high levels of risk may well have affected mental health.[35] The dubious efficacy of ancient medicine meant that the range of outcomes from illness was probably high, with much higher levels of resultant incapacity than today. In the modern world, chronic illness among the elderly is the most common form of affliction, whereas in ancient Rome it was acute sickness among the young. Few people lived long enough to worry about illnesses such as dementia. The typical death was not slow or lingering but the sudden result of a brief illness afflicting a young and seemingly healthy individual, and came as a shock to the victim's family.[36]

Comparative data from modern studies suggest we should find that gender-based inequalities were also reflected in differential exposure to risk.[37] Some references to the plight of women do occur in the ancient sources. In the famine at Amida in 546–7 CE, John of Ephesus noted the particular severity of 'the afflictions and suffering of mainly the poor, widows and orphans, who reached the verge of death'. Widows were generally left extremely vulnerable by the loss of their husbands, who would in most cases have been the main earner. Any situation that increased the difficulty of their situation could easily push them over the brink into destitution. Women are usually especially vulnerable in disasters that strike the domestic environment, as indeed are those in their care: children and sometimes the elderly. Any event, such as a daytime earthquake, striking when a greater proportion of women than men might be expected to have been within the confines of their homes, would probably have led to a far higher casualty rate among the female population than the male. In fact, though, we find little evidence of such gender differentials in

---

[35] I. Wilkinson, *Risk, Vulnerability and Everyday Life*, London: Routledge, 2008; on Roman mental health, see Toner, *Popular Culture in Ancient Rome*, Cambridge: Polity, 2009, pp. 54–91, and *Roman Disasters*, pp. 150–70.

[36] On the demography of the Roman world, see T. G. Parkin, *Demography and Roman Society*, Baltimore, MD: Johns Hopkins University Press, 1992, and W. Scheidel, *Death on the Nile: Disease and the Demography of Roman Egypt*, Mnemosyne Supplements, Leiden and Boston: Brill, 2001. On the Greek world, see R. Sallares, *The Ecology of the Ancient Greek World*, London: Duckworth, 1991.

[37] See E. Enarson and P. G. Dhar Chakrabarti, *Women, Gender and Disaster: Global Issues and Initiatives*, London: Sage, 2009; H. Rodríguez, E. L. Quarantelli, and R. R. Dynes (eds), *Handbook of Disaster Research*, New York: Springer, 2007, ch. 8, 'Gender and disaster: foundations and directions', pp. 130–46; A. Fothergill, 'Gender, risk, and disaster', *International Journal of Mass Emergencies and Disasters*, 14 (1996), 33–56. See Grey, 'Risk and vulnerability on the Campanian plain', on how social structures and environmental factors combine to create vulnerabilities to catastrophe.

Roman evidence, although the lack of evidence on these matters from the ancient world may simply reflect the gender bias in our sources. Male writers did not mention greater female mortality or morbidity because they either failed to notice it or did not think it important enough to record.

The risks individuals face are not simply the result of chance, completely beyond human influence. They also reflect the hierarchies of social life. The reason many of these risks rarely materialise in the most developed modern societies, and only have a modest impact when they do, is a function of those societies' vast expenditure of time and money on minimising both the risks to which their citizens are exposed and the effects on them when such exposure does occur. The Roman world was one in which far less public care was taken over its inhabitants. A high-risk context was the norm. Rome's social system therefore contributed significantly to this vulnerability. Negative events, such as food crises, reflected a lack of government interest and individual venality among the elite as much as harvest failures. Those in authority saw many sufferings as trivial distractions from the more serious matters of high politics. They had little abiding interest in the plight of the poor and the sick. This is not to say that the political leadership, and the social elite, did nothing to meet their needs in emergencies, but rather that the degree to which they took remedial action was limited and reflected an ideological choice based on a hierarchical view of the social world. The normality of suffering meant that the Roman government was largely able to ignore it. People did not on the whole blame those in authority for their plight, probably because they expected such events to happen from time to time.

Quantifying the level of risk the Romans faced is impossible. Ancient authors were not interested in providing accurate numerical evidence and lacked the means to do so even if they had been. This problematic nature of the evidence also makes it hard to discern any regular pattern of differential impact in the urban environment, where risks can be expected to have been higher. Urban environments tend to increase risks for the poorest because of the high density of population and the poor quality of housing. But the city of Rome's population was divided vertically not horizontally, meaning that areas of the city were less divided according to status and wealth than would now be the case. Modest multiple-occupancy residential buildings sat cheek-by-jowl with grand urban villas. Rome's infrastructure also provided some extra resilience, above all its large system of public food storage and a water supply via its aqueducts, and the fact that free or subsidised corn doles meant that the nutritional status of many may not have been as poor as might otherwise be expected.

One way of checking the reality of the Roman experience of risk vulnerability against our expectations based on comparative evidence is to examine the various reasons for death given by Roman tombstones.[38] Epitaphs represent a majority of all surviving inscriptions from the Roman world, with one estimate suggesting that of the 44,000 non-Christian inscriptions from the city of Rome at the time of the early empire, 28,000, or 61 per cent, were written to commemorate the dead. Of these, approximately 70 per cent were set up by freedmen. That so many were set up by former slaves is a testimony to how far the practice went down the social order. To be sure, we are mostly seeing the inscriptions of the better-off members of the non-elite – those who may have felt a stronger need to assert their identity owing to their earlier servile status – but we are still looking at a widespread phenomenon that gives an indication of the dangers faced in everyday Roman life.

In total, approximately 260 Latin grave inscriptions contain passages in which the cause of death is explicitly stated.[39] The largest group (eighty-five) are victims of war. This reflects the importance of inscriptions and memorialisation in the culture of the Roman military. The second-largest group (seventy-one) attests to victims of violent assault and robbery. Deaths from illness represent a significant group (eighteen). It is noteworthy how often the death is described as sudden. Sometimes the interventions of doctors are mentioned but they clearly failed to prevent the patient's demise. A dozen inscriptions record women who died during or immediately following childbirth. Veturia Grata, for example, died in her fourth pregnancy when only twenty-one years old. Or Rubria Festa, a provincial priestess, died at thirty-six, three days after giving birth to her tenth child, four of whom had predeceased her. Nine epitaphs commemorate those who had died in the arena, including the beast-fighter Maximinus, who died after being bitten by a leopard. Eight more attribute the deaths to deceit, poisoning and sorcery. Four tombs tell of victims of fire, including one member of the Praetorian Guard who died trying to extinguish a blaze in Ostia, whose citizens set up an epitaph to record their

---

[38] U. Ehmig, 'Subjektive und faktische Risiken: Votivgründe und Todesursachen in lateinischen Inschriften als Beispiele für Nachrichtenauswahl in der römischen Kaiserzeit', *Chiron*, 43 (2013), 127–98. Ehmig compares the causes of death on tombstones with the causes of anxiety recorded in votive inscriptions to see if perceptions of risk may have affected how the real level of underlying risk was seen. On the seasonal factors affecting mortality in the city of Rome, see W. Scheidel, 'Libitina's bitter gains: seasonal mortality and endemic disease in the ancient city of Rome', *Ancient Society*, 25 (1994), 151–75.

[39] On causes of death among children, see C. Laes, 'Children and accidents in Roman Antiquity', *Ancient Society*, 34 (2004), 153–70.

gratitude for his self-sacrifice. A large group of texts (twenty-two) tells of death by drowning, ten of which are stated as being in a shipwreck. Four epitaphs attest to deaths by falling, such as the twenty-one-year-old mosaic worker Hermas, who fell from a height while working. Others died as a result of accidents, with the fourteen-year-old Murra being killed by a friend's spear when practising the javelin.

When comparing this body of evidence with the risks we know ancient people faced, it is apparent that there is significant overlap. Disease, war, childbirth, shipwreck and accidents were the kinds of everyday risk that many people faced in their lives. It is striking how many were the victims of violent crime. This highlights the problem with this kind of evidence. In reality, death as a result of disease must have been the most common cause, especially when the young are included. But the social reality was that inscriptions were thought more worthy of older children and adults, of soldiers, mothers who had died doing their procreational duty and those who suffered dramatic fates at the hands of bandits and on the high seas. The number of victims of violent crime almost certainly overstates its frequency as a cause of death, reflecting what Ehmig calls its 'newsworthiness'. Quite how much it is overstated is impossible to say. Was death in this way a rarity that generated a high level of memorialisation? Or was it a fairly common, albeit shocking risk that threatened people all across the Roman world? The same is true of many of the epitaphs that record unusual or extreme situations that might touch the reader. A child dying in an accident with a spear grabbed the ancient reader's attention in a way that yet another infant mortality as a result of disease never could.

Imaginary Risk

Each society has its own set of fears and bogeymen. Social marginals such as outlaws generated a level of concern among a Roman audience that was in all likelihood out of kilter with the level of threat they actually posed. But such imaginary risks, as we might call them, generated a similar level of psychological insecurity as more concrete risks such as disease. What constitutes a risk is socially constructed, meaning that comparing risk levels in different societies is problematic. Certain issues are probably fairly universal – food, marriage plans, threats to physical safety – but others vary considerably in the degree of importance that people attach to them. As is so often the case in Roman society, status concerns ranked highly. A significant portion of the oracles and spells of the Roman world concerned the removal of perceived and actual threats to status, opportunities for status advancement and gaining revenge for actions by social competitors that had resulted in a loss of face.[40] This was a society where 'risk was other people'.[41]

The danger that constitutes a risk need not be real, and many of the threats the Romans faced were neither material nor physical. Above all, they feared the gods and what they might do. Offending the gods could threaten the *pax deorum* – literally the peace of the gods or the compact struck between gods and mankind – on which Roman prosperity ultimately depended. Religious pollution through improper rituals or behaviour could generate a swift divine retribution in the form of natural disasters or military defeat. Many self-reported dangers in the ancient world reflect this significant conceptual difference between what the modern world and the Romans thought represented a risk to the social order. Religious and moral ideas were often central to their thinking.

How then can we compare, let alone quantify, the degree of risk that different societies face? Beck's argument that modernity faces a higher level of risk than existed in the pre-modern word has some appeal but is hard to maintain when we see the size, range and types of risks that afflicted the Romans. Is it possible to add up all these various risks to reach a societal total? Again, it might seem theoretically achievable but the practical difficulties are immense. And how can we compare the risk of nuclear war with the fear generated by the gods – two very different but potentially overwhelming forms of power that can both create significant anxiety? In many ways, the level of everyday risk faced by the inhabitants of modernity is extremely low in comparison with that of the Roman world, and it is only the perception of them that has intensified. It is certainly the case that the modern world has seen a significant rise in risk discourse; that is to say, a way of dealing with the uncertainties of the future by means of a quantifying approach. But it is possible that the very act of carrying out these calculations has served only to increase the public's awareness of the uncertainties that they have to live with and to exaggerate their fears about them.

---

[40] On risks in social situations, see C. R. Sunstein, *Laws of Fear: Beyond the Precautionary Principle*, Cambridge: Cambridge University Press, 2005.
[41] Eidinow, *Oracles, Curses, and Risk*, p. 231.

CHAPTER 3

A Risk Culture

Hacking has argued that the calculating concept of risk started 'to dominate instinct, tradition, and collective wisdom, in a measured way, only in seventeenth-century Europe'. Before the Renaissance, Bernstein claims, 'people perceived the future as little more than a matter of luck or the result of random variations, and most of their decisions were driven by instinct'.[1] Chapter 2 argued that the Romans did not see the future as purely a matter of chance, nor indeed as a matter of predestination. This chapter sets out to challenge the view that a sharp distinction can be drawn between the modern calculating concept of risk and the practices of tradition and the operation of instinct.

All humans have to cope with various types of uncertainty, which reflects their ignorance about the future. There are areas where individuals are consciously ignorant about certain future events. There are other beliefs that reflect a kind of tacit or unconscious knowledge about the future that is learned 'at the mother's knee'. Then there are future outcomes that are not even imaginable. This chapter deals with the second of these in the Roman world: the cultural attitudes, tactics and beliefs that helped them cope with the dangers they faced. Most of these problems had arisen before and could be addressed by practices that people had learned through tradition. This knowledge represented a ready-made set of tools to help people address most of the troubles that were likely to come their way. One of the main problems individuals confronted in Antiquity was that they had only very limited knowledge on which to base their decisions. Indeed, Horden and Purcell suggest that 'decision-making under uncertainty' characterises the whole Mediterranean micro-ecology.[2] By relying

---

[1] I. Hacking, 'Risk and dirt', in Doyle and Ericson, *Risk and Morality*, pp. 22–47, p. 27; Bernstein, *Against the Gods*, p. 18.
[2] See P. Horden and N. Purcell, *The Corrupting Sea: A Study of Mediterranean History*, Oxford: Blackwell, 2000, p. 522.

A Risk Culture

on trusted techniques, they were able to cope better with this handicap because it allowed them to utilise the collective wisdom that had been accumulated over generations.[3]

I am terming this a 'risk culture'. In other words, it is not a risk society, as Beck defines modernity, because these Roman ways of coping contained a lower level of individuality, consciousness or reflexivity. Being mostly inherited, a risk culture reflected the accumulated experience of previous Romans that was hardwired into their practical actions concerning uncertainty. It included what we might term 'intuition', which we can interpret not so much as an innate knowledge but as an instinctive response based upon experience and received understanding.

The term culture also highlights that, unlike in Beck's *Risk Society*, there was often no straightforward divide between expert and lay knowledge.[4] Modernity has been sceptical about lay people's ability to deal with risk, usually seeing them as lacking the intellectual skills to make difficult decisions or basing them upon irrational assumptions. It has been argued that lay people tend to see familiar or voluntary risks as less serious than risks that are new or imposed upon them, and they are more likely to be concerned about risks that are rare and memorable than those that are seen as commonplace but less destructive.[5] Lay knowledge of risk also tends to be highly contextualised and localised, often based upon everyday empirical experience, and highly sceptical of outsiders who by definition lack the same level of local expertise. These biases lead lay people to draw erroneous conclusions compared to statistical models.[6] Of course, the Roman world had no statistical models to compare with lay knowledge. But the Roman evidence does show that lay approaches were generally culturally rooted forms of collective knowledge.[7] These were widely seen as powerful primarily because of their foundation in experience. People knew that they worked, at least to some extent. The Romans did, however, have approaches to dealing with uncertainty which display a higher level of

---

[3] On risk and risk-control strategies, see Toner, *Popular Culture in Ancient Rome*, pp. 11–53; and in the modern world, Tulloch and Lupton, *Risk and Everyday Life*.

[4] The literature on 'culture' is vast but see M. Carrithers, *Why Humans Have Cultures: Explaining Anthropology and Social Diversity*, Oxford: Oxford University Press, 1992, and C. Geertz, *The Interpretation of Cultures: Selected Essays*, New York: Basic Books, 1973.

[5] P. Slovic, 'Perception of risk', *Science*, 236 (1987), 280–5. Such views assume that risk avoidance is rational, that all humans are rational agents seeking to avoid risk and that lay views are biases away from the 'neutral' stance of experts.

[6] D. Dörner, *The Logic of Failure: Recognizing and Avoiding Error in Complex Situations*, trans. R. and R. Kimber, Reading, MA: Addison-Wesley, 1996.

[7] On lay approaches to risk, see B. Wynne, 'May the sheep safely graze?', in S. Lash, B. Szerszinski and B. Wynne (eds), *Risk, Environment and Modernity*, London: Sage, 1996, pp. 44–83.

conscious understanding and relied more on expert knowledge in various fields, such as the law, logistics, finance and oracles, and these are the subject of Chapter 4. To some extent, this is an arbitrary divide since all these approaches display varying degrees of self-awareness, but I think it is useful to highlight that the Romans used a combination of inherited and more technical strategies for dealing with an uncertain future.

The Roman world exposed its citizens to a variety of risks, but the accumulated experience of coping with these represented a form of mutual mitigation of danger. That people thought it was worth taking measures to protect future states shows that something important was at stake, whether it was social status, health or money, and that some element of human planning was thought capable of affecting the outcome. The Romans recognised that these areas were too significant to be left to fate or simple chance, even if the limitations of human agency were widely acknowledged. Today, risk is generally used to focus on situations where a negative outcome might happen, which probably reflects the psychology of risk: that when faced with the consequentiality of risk people tend to focus on the downside. In the Roman world, where even middling sorts 'lived under a permanent threat of impoverishment',[8] it is not surprising that we also find this skew to the negative. The Romans faced a whole range of risks, from crop failure to climatic volatility, from loss of status to violent crime, all of which entailed the adoption of risk management strategies to help them cope. Some of these will have produced only a marginal effect at best, but the Romans inhabited a world where even small improvements could have a major impact on the quality of life of the individual. Peasants were risk-averse for good reason. Their risk culture helped them survive in a world which was full of dangers, both real and imaginary, about which the state lacked the capacity or interest to help. In this chapter I draw on the work that has been done in this area to ask: what were the main features of this risk culture?

Pragmatism

Surviving books of oracles and astrology are useful in that they show us the issues that Romans felt sufficiently concerned about to consult the gods. The headings of the late first-century CE astrologer Dorotheus of Sidon's work run as follows: runaways, asking from rulers, freeing slaves, buying

[8] P. Brown, *Poverty and Leadership in the Later Roman Empire*, Lebanon, NH: University Press of New England, 2002, p. 14.

land or slaves, building, demolishing, hiring, pregnancy, partnerships, marriage, buying animals, buying and selling, wills, illness, surgery, medicine, spirits, when to start something, arguments, property, travel, the sick, chains, letters, building ships, debt and eyes.[9] Similarly, the second-century CE Oracles of Astrampsychus list ninety-two questions to put to the gods. The topics include relationships, money, travel, health, work, business, inheritance and public posts. Many of the questions imply a male questioner, none a female one. By contrast, the cult of Diana at Aricia was popular with women and reflected more of their concerns, such as childbirth, education, love and healing.[10] It is noticeable that the range of topics is practical and focused on self-interest.[11] Many of them could be termed everyday, but even then they represent the larger decisions of daily life, which would have a meaningful impact on the questioner. They are also focused on what we might call regular risks, such as travel and health, rather than on any remote risk.

Poverty bred a need to be practical. Or, as the Roman proverb put it, 'poverty is the sister to good sense'. Proverbs provide a good example of the knowledge that informed a risk culture. Compact and memorable, they offered practical wisdom on a wide variety of issues in a form that was not linked to any particular context.[12] They covered a similar range of 'daily life' problems: birth, marriage, children and death, as well as providing practical strategies for dealing with authority and the powerful. People believed in them partly because of their tradition, partly because they represented a communal wisdom. Risks were often expressed in metaphorical terms. So the saying '*hic abundant leones*' (lions abound here) used an animal synonymous with ferocity as a way to symbolise a place of unknown dangers. Similarly, '*auribus teneo lupum*' (I'm holding a wolf by the ears) reflected a situation that was a difficult balancing act, where the danger was very hard to control. Clearly, lions and wolves here reflect the outlook of a traditional rural way of life. They display a conservatism

---

[9] See Pingree, D. (ed.), *Dorothei Sidonii Carmen astrologicum: interpretationem Arabicam in linguam Anglicam versam una cum Dorothei fragmentis et Graecis et Latinis*, Leipzig: Teubner, 1976.
[10] See C. M. C. Green, *Roman Religion and the Cult of Diana at Aricia*, Cambridge: Cambridge University Press, 2007.
[11] As Klingshirn says of the later *sortes sangallenses*, 'for the most part, it warns clients to look out for their own good fortune, to make decisions on the basis of aggressive self-interest'. W, Klingshirn, 'Christian divination in late Roman Gaul: the *Sortes Sangallenses*', in Johnston and Struck, *Mantikê*, pp. 99–128, p. 112.
[12] On the theory of proverbs, see J. Obelkevich, 'Proverbs and social history', in P. Burke and R. Porter (eds), *The Social History of Language*, Cambridge: Cambridge University Press, 1987, pp. 43–72; for the Roman tradition, see T. Morgan, *Popular Morality in the Early Roman Empire*, Cambridge: Cambridge University Press, 2007.

that sees good advice as being permanent and universal. Unsentimental and resolutely practical, they emphasise the importance of individual action and self-reliance. They are also full of fears: fear of destitution, fear of competitive neighbours, fear of the powerful. Proverbs paint, as Morgan says, 'a picture of a society dominated by inequality, hostility and fear'.[13]

Proverbs also offered a flexible way to consider problems from different angles. Contradictions between different sayings did not reflect incoherence but suggested alternative ways of dealing with particular problems. This enabled the individual to consider two different courses of action and then decide which was more likely to produce a better outcome. This is inherently probabilistic thinking and involved active decision-taking, even if the likelihood of particular outcomes was in no way quantified.

Diversification

Diversification offered a key way to deal with living in an environment dominated by uncertainty and vulnerability. The Mediterranean climate produces high levels of agricultural volatility, with annual average variations in crop yield in excess of 60 per cent in Tunisia.[14] The volatility in the climate meant that farmers would use astronomy to pinpoint exactly where they stood in the seasonal cycle to help them predict the weather, but the success of such strategies could only have been modest.[15] Spreading risk meant that any potential harm could be limited, even if it reduced the potential return. Peasants sowed a variety of crops, if possible in different microclimatic zones, in order to reduce the risk of total harvest failure.[16] Crops would also have to be selected according to the availability of resources. Growing vines or olive trees could be expected to generate a higher level of return than subsistence crops but required a significant investment of both time and money and could easily fail. Cato therefore advises growing a wide variety of crops, from olives, grapes and figs to vetch and pulses, as well as maintaining woods for timber. Younger family

---

[13] Ibid., p. 82.   [14] See Horden and Purcell, *The Corrupting Sea*, p. 152.
[15] See D. Lehoux, *Astronomy, Weather, and Calendars in the Ancient World: Parapegmata and Related Texts in Classical and Near-Eastern Societies*, Cambridge: Cambridge University Press, 2007. It was not just farmers who relied on the regular movements of the stars to locate themselves seasonally but also sailors, soldiers and travellers.
[16] See P. Halstead and J. O'Shea, *Bad Year Economics: Cultural Responses to Risk and Uncertainty*, Cambridge: Cambridge University Press, 1989. On Roman peasant culture, see Bowes, K. (ed.), *The Roman Peasant Project 2009–2014: Excavating the Roman Rural Poor*, University Museum monograph, 154, Philadelphia: University of Pennsylvania Museum of Archaeology and Anthropology, 2020.

members might also be sent out to work as apprentices to provide a valuable additional income from a source less correlated with agricultural returns. These decisions represented a dynamic and adaptive response to variations in the climatic outlook or other factors that might impact on the expected harvest. Most of these were known risks, such as low rainfall and other such regular events that could reduce crop yields, and the peasants were able to react based on the accumulated knowledge that had been handed down from their forefathers. The overall impact was to create a buffer zone between the individual and any potentially negative outcome, since it was less likely to affect all different sources of income equally.

This distribution of crop yields in the Mediterranean does not exhibit a normal, bell-shaped distribution curve but rather displays kurtosis or 'fat tails'. A normal distribution tells us to expect two-thirds of outcomes to be within one standard deviation of the average, but in the ancient world the climate meant that extreme outcomes, sometimes significantly outside this standard deviation, happened far more regularly than would statistically be expected. Bumper harvests could easily be followed by years of dearth. Peasants had an urgent need, therefore, to ensure they had put by sufficient surpluses to cope with these shortages. Estimating how much of a surplus was required involved calculations concerning how much could be spared, how much could be safely stored and how great a shortfall might occur in the future, all of which involved weighing up likely outcomes based on what had happened in the past.

Particularly extreme events were likely to exceed the ability of surpluses to compensate for shortfalls. In such situations, more extreme strategies would be employed. Eusebius' account of a famine, which had been aggravated by the onset of plague, describes how some bartered their possessions for food or substituted usual foodstuffs for alternatives and 'injured their bodily health and died from chewing small wisps of hay and recklessly eating certain pernicious herbs'. Even well-born women were driven to beg in the marketplaces.[17] Likewise, the historian Joshua the Stylite describes a famine of 500–1 CE during which the rural poor were forced to abandon their home areas in the search for food. Those left behind became increasingly desperate and went so far as to 'cut off the inedible bits from dead carcasses and boiled and ate them'. By the following year, those in the villages were 'eating vetches, and others were roasting and eating shrivelled grapes', while those in the city roamed the streets, 'picking out and eating the dung-spattered roots and leaves of vegetables'.

---

[17] Eusebius, *Church History* 9.8.

Everywhere, there were children and infants, some of whose mothers had died, others of whom had been abandoned when they had asked their mothers for something to eat but who, having nothing to give, had fled.[18] This was an event so extreme that most could not have afforded to put aside enough resources to cope with it. It was also something that was highly unusual. Planning for such extreme risks is always problematic. Knowing that a remote possibility would require the allocation of significant resources is likely to lead to it being seen as a risk that can be ignored.

Financial Management

The majority of the Roman population can be described as 'shallow poor', meaning that they had enough resources or savings to cope with typical shortfalls in harvest or income but not with more extreme situations. Comparative evidence suggests that this category comprised perhaps 70 per cent of all people.[19] Living at a modest level above subsistence meant that financial management had to be taken seriously. Most importantly, this meant maximising sources of income. The poet Juvenal describes a father advising his son on how to make a living:

> You should make some goods which you can sell at more than 50 per cent profit, and don't be overcome with disgust at the type of merchandise which has to be relegated to the other side of the Tiber [by which he means tanned leather goods], or think that you should make any distinction between perfumes and animal hides: profit smells sweet, no matter what goods it comes from.[20]

This is obviously the exaggerated view of a satirist but it gives a sense of the pressure to make money. Making money was hard work. When recommending a young man to a friend, the younger Pliny notes that 'he loves hard work as much as poor people usually do'.[21] Unskilled labourers would always be vulnerable to the economic cycle. Craftsmen were able to reduce this vulnerability by specialising in a trade. Even then, trades such as these were 'hard work and could scarcely provide just enough',[22] and any meaningful downturn would have seen their business fall also.

---

[18] *The Chronicle of Pseudo-Joshua the Stylite* 38–42 in *The Chronicle of Pseudo-Joshua the Stylite*, trans. F. R. Trombley and J. W. Watt, Liverpool: Liverpool University Press, 2000.

[19] See Brown, *Poverty and Leadership in the Later Roman Empire*, p. 15. On poverty, see also M. Atkins and R. Osborne (eds), *Poverty in the Roman World*, Cambridge: Cambridge University Press, 2006, and F. Carlà-Uhink, L. Cecchet and C. A. Machado (eds), *Poverty in Ancient Greece and Rome*, Abingdon: Routledge, 2022.

[20] Juvenal, *Satire* 14.200–5.   [21] Pliny, *Letters* 7.22.   [22] Lucian, *Fugitives* 12–13.

Women contributed to the household economy by manufacturing household goods, weaving cloth and producing and preserving food, as well as cleaning, mending and washing. They could also improve household incomes and seem to have worked primarily in areas such as the service sector, spinning wool, making jewellery, serving in taverns, hairdressing and making and mending clothes.[23] Families were vulnerable to food price inflation as it constituted such a large part of their weekly spend. If the family income was unable to buy food, then one response was to move. As the moral to one of Aesop's fables says, 'the poor, being unencumbered, easily move from city to city'.[24]

Family Management

Family life helped bring security in a number of ways. Children served as both insurance scheme and pension provider, ideally ensuring that parents were looked after in old age or incapacity. Children could also be sent out to work at an early age, with somewhere between five and ten being the most common age for a non-elite child.[25] But family life also generated risks. Family management was vital if the domestic unit was to maximise its resistance to shocks and smooth the volatility of its income and expenditure. Risk was highest when most of the family group's income came from the same source. For this reason women were exceptionally vulnerable, as the husband for most families was the main bread-winner.[26]

Children brought costs with them in the years before they could generate any extra income. This meant that the head of the family had to control the number of children to ensure there were sufficient resources, even when taking into account the likelihood that a number of children could be expected to die young. Desperate times might mean selling children into slavery or to a begging gang, who would mutilate them to increase their begging power.[27] There were no effective means of contraception, although various abortifacients offered a potentially dangerous and unreliable means of terminating unwanted pregnancies. Alternatively,

---

[23] S. Treggiari, 'Lower class women in the Roman economy', *Florilegium*, 1 (1979), 65–86.
[24] Aesop, *Fable* 228.
[25] *Digest* 7.7.6.1 has children working by five. See K. R. Bradley, *Discovering the Roman Family: Studies in Roman Social History*, Oxford: Oxford University Press, 1991, pp. 114–16.
[26] See esp. A. R. Parkin, *Poverty in the Early Roman Empire: Ancient and Modern Conceptions and Constructs*, unpublished PhD dissertation, Cambridge University, 2001, ch. 4; and '"You do him no service": an exploration of pagan almsgiving', in Atkins and Osborne, *Poverty in the Roman World*, pp. 60–82.
[27] Seneca the Elder, *Controversies* 10.4.16.

family planning could take place after birth. Infants could be disposed of by exposure or infanticide, and Seneca describes how some fathers would simply throw out weak and deformed babies.[28] The first-century CE philosopher Musonius Rufus, in his text entitled *Should Every Child That Is Born Be Raised?*, argues against those who cite poverty as a reason not to raise children, which suggests that this was a reasonably common attitude. It is worth noting, however, that such a fate was not reserved for the unwanted children of the poor, and Rufus describes how it is not just the poor who expose infants, 'but those who have an abundance of things', which they do in order that 'those previously born might be more prosperous', a practice he describes as 'monstrous'.[29] But for the poor, these various methods of family management could limit their vulnerability to a lack of food or a reduction in income. The decisions involved conscious assessments about how many children was enough. They were also not innovations but rather standard practices that were socially tolerated, if not endorsed.

Social Relations

Social contacts were also a way to reduce vulnerability to risk. Networks of friends, kin and neighbours could all act as a kind of insurance policy against hard times.[30] Some of this work was done between the men of the household, at public events and through business ventures. The women were also expected to do a great deal of the work in maintaining such reciprocal relations, and, by keeping up daily contacts and ensuring the proper observance of various social niceties, they established a support network that could be turned to for help in times of distress.

We have an imaginary example of how such support networks operated, written by Alciphron, in the second century CE, and representing an appeal from one farmer to another:

> A violent hailstorm has sheared off our standing grain, and there is nothing left to keep us from famine. Because we have no money we cannot buy imported wheat. But I hear that you have something left over from last year's good harvest. So please lend me twenty bushels, to give me the means to save my own life and that of my wife and children. And when a year of

---

[28] Ibid.
[29] *Lectures* 15B. cf. Polybius, *Histories* 36.17.5–10 on how the Greeks limited family size to one or two children.
[30] On the later empire, see Grey, *Constructing Communities in the Late Roman Countryside*, esp. pp. 58–74 on risk and reciprocity.

good harvest comes along, we will repay you. Please do not let good neighbours go to ruin in times such as these.[31]

From the recipient's point of view, this letter would have provoked a thoroughgoing risk assessment before any wheat would be sent: could the wheat be spared? Was the relationship strong enough to warrant it? Could they repay? Would they repay? Reciprocity was never a simple matter. It relied upon many levels of assessment, even if this was carried out in an instinctive rather than numerical way.

Social interaction could mitigate potential future shortages, but also had to deal with the fallout of living in a competitive world. Attitudes to surplus and shortfall reflected the notion of the 'limited good', which saw the world as a zero-sum game.[32] For an individual to succeed, by definition another must fail, since it reflected an underlying belief that there was a fixed amount of wealth to go round. This also implied that a person's misfortune occurred as the direct result of another's gain and vice versa. We can see this in Artemidorus' interpretation of dreaming of brothers as having 'the same meaning as enemies, for they do not contribute to a person's welfare but rather his impoverishment' because they divide any inheritance.[33] This resulted in a world full of squabbles and conflicts, and many fables and proverbs warn about the problems of fighting with neighbours and the inconstancy of friends. In that sense, risk was understood in a personalised form which necessitated a range of direct social interventions in order to mitigate it. This might include gossip and slander to try to tarnish a rival's reputation, or public accusations of immoral acts to try and force offenders to change their ways, or writing graffiti to warn others about various forms of antisocial behaviour.

The Management of Social Superiors

Romans also sought security by turning to vertical social links, in the form of patrons and the authorities. The benefits granted by social superiors to those lower down the social scale ranged from assistance in providing extra food during shortages to more everyday benefits in the form of public banquets, games and festivals.[34] We have many examples of the elite

---

[31] *Letter* 2.3 quoted in B. Shaw, 'Our daily bread', *Social History of Medicine*, 2 (1989), 205–13, p. 205 with minor changes.
[32] See G. M. Foster, 'Peasant society and the image of limited good', *American Anthropologist*, 67 (1965), 293–315.
[33] Artemidorus, *The Interpretation of Dreams* 4.70.
[34] On food aid, see Garnsey, *Famine and Food Supply*, pp. 58–63.

providing disaster relief. When the amphitheatre collapsed in Fidenae, Tacitus tells us that 'the great houses were thrown open', and dressings and doctors were supplied to all comers.[35] Local leaders were expected to make the most of their connections to address such serious problems, and the weight of this expectation generally seems to have worked. The fact that food crises were common but famines rare suggests that these social mechanisms were reasonably effective in alleviating shortfalls in the harvest.[36]

The elite responded to such social pressure because it gave them an opportunity to display their status and enhance their prestige. Many honorific inscriptions mention the generosity of local officials or private individuals during food shortages when they provided subsidised grain to ordinary people. Such gift-giving also offered a means for members of the elite to compete among themselves and establish their local reputation for leadership. We can get a sense of what people expected from their leaders in the election slogans that were painted on the walls in Pompeii, commending candidates as 'most worthy citizens' and for having 'done many things generously'. Some spell it out plainly: 'he will do something for you'.[37] The provision of aid served to legitimise the very social inequality that generated it.

The elite gave assistance in order to prevent any widespread social disquiet and understood that riots could easily erupt if they failed to respond to food shortages. When problems arose with the grain supply in Rome, Tacitus describes how protests broke out that 'were more frequent and more outspoken than usual' and, in a later food crisis, an angry crowd went so far as to manhandle the emperor Claudius.[38] A commonly held suspicion maintained that the wealthy elite often caused food shortages by hoarding supplies in order to raise prices. During a food shortage in fourth-century CE Antioch, the crowd in the theatre shouted: 'Nothing is scarce, but nothing is cheap.' Regardless of the truth of the claim, the emperor Julian directed the city's elite to sort out the problem by rejecting 'unfair profits'.[39] E. P. Thompson argued with reference to early modern England that a strong sense of popular morality could be discerned in protests of this kind.[40] The people believed in a fair price for bread and the authorities were obliged to police the market so that it

---

[35] Tacitus, *Annals* 4.63. [36] See Garnsey, *Famine and Food Supply*, pp. 1–39. [37] *CIL* 4.429.
[38] Tacitus, *Annals* 6.13, 12.43. [39] Julian, *Beard-Hater* 368C.
[40] E. P. Thompson, 'The moral economy of the English crowd in the eighteenth century', *Past & Present*, 50 (1971), 76–136.

operated fairly. As such, the people believed in a 'moral economy'. Food protests reflected a traditional view of social reciprocity between the rulers and the ruled, and popular anger erupted when this established social contract was broken. It represented a communal mechanism for limiting the serious threat posed by food shortages.

Dealing with the powerful itself posed a significant risk for the ordinary citizens of Rome. 'There are as many tyrants as there are local officials', complains the Christian writer Salvian in the later empire.[41] The authorities could not be relied upon to deal with complainants fairly, as the Evangelist Luke warns:

> When you go with your accuser before a magistrate, on the way you should make an effort to settle the case, or you might be dragged before the judge, and the judge will hand you over to the officer, and the officer will throw you in prison. I tell you, you will never get out until you have paid every last penny.[42]

The fable of the ass who hunted with the lion warns, 'do not form an alliance nor go into any kind of partnership with a man more powerful than yourself'.[43] But the powerful could not be avoided entirely since they represented an important source of benefits, particularly, as we have seen, in times of crisis. Such patrons had to be dealt with carefully so as to ensure that the weak did not expose themselves to undue risks.

Patrons were managed by means of deference and flattery. Apuleius notes the deference (*verecundia*) of the poor for the rich.[44] They assumed a hesitating, risk-averse stance, watching attentively for any tell-tale signs of mood change in the patron and shaping their language to avoid giving any offence. Anthropologists have noted that a common cultural practice is for members of dominated groups or the lower levels of society to 'express deference to dominant members by bumbling ... and [the] language of slow-wittedness or buffoonery'.[45] Such humility in the presence of superiors showed the elite that the poor knew their place. It kept the wealthy well disposed to offering benefits because it gave them what they wanted out of the bargain: respect and an acknowledgement of their high status. It served to legitimate their position in their own eyes. Some of the financial benefits donated by the emperors could be significant. Julius

---

[41] *On the Government of God* 5.4 quot curiales tot tyranni.   [42] 12:58–9.   [43] Babrius 67.
[44] Apuleius, *Metamorphoses* 9.35.
[45] S. C. Levinson and P. Brown, *Politeness: Some Universals in Language Usage*, Cambridge: Cambridge University Press, 1987, p. 186; on deference among elite Romans, see J. E. Lendon, *Empire of Honour: The Art of Government in the Roman World*, Oxford: Clarendon, 1997, pp. 57–63.

Caesar and Augustus both gave large handouts of money to the citizens of Rome from their personal fortunes, and by the time of Marcus Aurelius, when he returned to Rome in 177 CE after some years away campaigning on the northern frontiers, the pressure generated by the urban plebs combined with an imperial need to be seen as generous resulted in his awarding them each an unprecedented eight gold coins.[46]

An inscription from Forlì in Italy recounts the life story of a man nicknamed 'farmer', who, through years of effort, had risen from the ranks of the slave gangs to become the master of his own household. 'Take all this as true advice', he says, 'whoever wants to live really well and freely: first, show respect where it is due; next, want what's best for your master; honour your parents; earn others' trust; don't speak or listen to slander. If you don't harm or betray anyone you will lead a pleasant life, uprightly and happily, giving no offence.'[47] This was the kind of risk-averse attitude towards social relations that was often needed to survive in the Roman world.

Religion

Like most inhabitants of pre-industrial societies, the Romans sought to understand and cope with the uncertainties of the future by means of religious ideas which explained the order and functioning of the universe. Religion suffused ancient life. The Roman state took advice from a variety of expert priests, whose job was to explain the signs given by the gods. The examination of chicken entrails was a core part of the state's decision-making process, as was the monitoring of occurrences of thunder and lightning.[48] Prodigies could be explained by consulting soothsayers or asking the magistrates known as the decemvirs to consult the Sibylline Books. At an everyday level, people kissed their hands to the gods as they passed sacred places and statues, and they would often carry a small effigy of their favourite god on their person.[49] Just as people tried to protect themselves by building various forms of human relationships, so they sought to establish a variety of links with the divine that could act as a buffer against dangers that might arise. They would also seek to avoid

---

[46] Dio Cassius 72.32.1.
[47] *CIL* 11.600 quoted in R. MacMullen, *Roman Social Relations, 50 B.C. to A.D. 284*, New Haven, CT: Yale University Press, 1974, p. 44, with minor alterations to his free translation.
[48] See J. Scheid, *An Introduction to Roman Religion*, trans. J. Lloyd, Edinburgh: Edinburgh University Press, 2003, pp. 112–17.
[49] Apuleius, *Apology* 56; Minucius Felix, *Octavius* 2.4.

doing anything that might upset the divine. The elder Pliny noted that many Romans would not cut their nails on market days, in silence or beginning with the forefinger.[50] It is easy to dismiss these various forms of religious activity as irrational superstition. But religion established a consistent approach to dealing with danger by offering a variety of rites to ward off trouble. Belief in the gods and various supernatural spirits explained why humans suffered so many travails, with divine power being understood to be amoral and ubiquitous, affecting all manner of human activities. But it also offered a means for mortals to do something to influence divine behaviour and thereby alter outcomes in the human sphere. Through rituals, rites and magic, the divine could be nudged to act in a way that their worshippers desired. Like patronage, it was undoubtedly a relationship between unequals, but that did not mean the weak had no influence over future outcomes.

In her study on oracles and curses in Classical Greece, Eidinow notes that these represented strategies by which ordinary men and women, individually and collectively, 'expressed and managed aspects of the uncertainty and risk of everyday life', and it is highly likely that the shared experience of living in the Mediterranean climate meant that most Romans used such religious tools in the same way. In the face of uncertainty and confronted with making difficult decisions, oracles enabled people to feel sure they were making the right choice and so avoid situations where they would be at risk. Curses, on the other hand, tried to change the odds of such negative events happening in the first place. Religious rituals of this kind also provided an outlet for social competitiveness. When faced with social opponents, curses offered a way 'to limit the damage their enemies might inflict'. As Eidinow says, this was a society 'riddled with rumour, beset by envy, suspicion, and rivalry'. Curse tablets therefore provided a means of a pre-emptive strike against such perceived risk.[51]

Texts as geographically varied as the Greek Magical Papyri from Egypt and the Bath curse tablets show how this was a religious practice that spread across the empire. The texts are highly formulaic, probably in an attempt to establish a sense of authority and tradition. The inscriptions from Bath therefore contain the same strange phrases and *voces magicae* as those from other ends of the empire. They also share the same aggressive verbal violence, generally directed against social rivals and those that have harmed the spell's author. One example, from North Africa, expresses a profound sense of powerlessness in the face of a life dominated by

---

[50] Pliny, *Natural History* 28.5.   [51] Eidinow, *Oracles, Curses, and Risk*, pp. 4–5, 231.

malevolent forces, malevolently directed: 'Here lies Ennia Fructuosa' a wife of 'unmistakable modesty' and 'unusual loyalty'. She married at fifteen and died at twenty-eight but 'she did not receive the kind of death she deserved – cursed by spells, she long lay mute so that her life was rather torn from her by violence than given back to nature'. Fructuosa's husband, Aelius, a tribune in the Third Legion, set up the inscription so that 'either the infernal gods or the heavenly deities will punish this wicked crime'.[52] It is, of course, possible to see this as reflecting a fatalistic attitude to life, where human agency was minimal. But the act of writing the spell also exhibits a belief that it was possible to elicit some form of divine retribution for the assault that a human rival had unleashed against her.

Magic of this kind can be seen as symptomatic of a society where local bitterness might dominate social interactions. Magic in this context did no more than help people keep danger at arm's length or, at best, turn any curse back against its sender. One defensive spell from Pontus, in modern Turkey, reads: 'Drive away the curse from Rouphina; and if someone does me an injustice, send the curse back against him. And don't let poison harm me.'[53] Such spells give us some sense of the psychology that lay behind this kind of magic. Rouphina assumes that the likelihood that someone is out to curse her is great enough for her to take the trouble to make a prophylactic counter-curse. Of course, we do not know the full story here, and it may be she had good reason to be afraid. Even so, it is interesting that she assumes her attacker would be using supernatural means to target her and that this prompts her to react. The fear of physical attack in the form of poison is almost an afterthought – it is the supernatural forces of the spell that most terrify her. Spells such as these show that individuals were prepared to take active steps to help manage the threats they faced and reveal an outlook that was in many ways neatly shaped to the competitive environment in which it operated.

Religion was also widely believed to diminish the risk of illness. Illness was regularly seen, not as a physiological process, but as an invasion of the body by demonic forces. Medical doctors, such as Galen, who looked for physical causes for ill-health were rare. In reality, ancient medicine encompassed a huge array of different types of knowledge and practice, many of which involved potions derived from traditional folklore, or practices that we would see as religious in character. Votive offerings were the staple

---

[52] J. G. Gager (ed.), *Curse Tablets and Binding Spells from the Ancient World*, Oxford: Oxford University Press, 1992, p. 246.
[53] Ibid., pp. 225–6

expression of individual religiosity, and articulated popular fears concerning an enormous range of afflictions and illnesses. Hundreds of these clay images have been found in the river Tiber, where it runs through Rome – often depicting internal organs, frequently the uterus – and these offerings were also used in healing cults such as that of Asclepius on the Tiber island.[54] Items such as amulets and apotropaic phalluses were also commonly employed to help ward off evil spirits. These served as a form of risk control adopted for the purposes of reducing susceptibility to illness and for maintaining well-being, all of which contradicts any image we might have of a people passively resigned to their fate.

Scepticism comes readily when we consider Roman 'experts'. For us, ancient magicians could not have performed miracles. While this is true, the ancient belief in their efficacy may have produced some placebo effect. It also seems to have produced a change of behaviour in some. Numbers of confessional inscriptions from second- and third-century Lydia and Phrygia, in what is now Turkey, were set up by people who thought they had been targeted by magic, and had decided to return items they had previously stolen because they had then suffered the kind of illness or misfortune often requested in curse tablets. But aside from this, a lack of efficacy does not detract from the fact that the Romans consulted an array of such religious experts. Many religious activities were characterised by having cheap and easy access, and non-exclusivity, in that making use of the services of one did not preclude the use of another. We can interpret the use of multiple approaches to the divine as a form of diversification, in order to minimise the risk of one route failing to deliver assistance. While a belief in the Fates coexisted alongside such religious experts, their claims to knowledge expressed a belief that a variety of divine factors were at play at any one time and that divination was a way for people to gain some understanding of future events. It was 'a tool for individuals to gain some grip on the future' and how 'fears about the future were turned into hope'.[55]

A Belief in Luck

Just as the ancients did not see their life as simply governed by fate, neither did they see it as a matter of random chance. Fortuna could be influenced in the same way as other divine forces. We can term this a belief in luck:

---

[54] J. Rüpke, *Religion of the Romans*, trans. R. Gordon, Cambridge: Polity, 2007, pp. 154–73.
[55] Beerden, *Worlds Full of Signs*, p. 221.

the idea that the laws of chance, which dictate that events will even out over the long term, can be overcome. Of course, the Romans lacked an understanding of these laws. For them, it was obvious that some people were luckier than others, and they perceived this as a reflection of divine favour. It is why they had no separate terms for chance and luck, both being represented by the goddess Fortuna (Tyche in Greek). But we can see their beliefs regarding how this divine power could be influenced as representing an ancient body of knowledge for coping with and compensating for 'the problems associated with decision making when indeterminacy predominates'. It was a form of 'luck epistemics' that enabled them to manage the uncertain and the unknown.[56]

According to the dream interpreter Artemidorus, to dream of the goddess Tyche, chance, standing upon a rolling ball is 'inauspicious for all men because of the precariousness of the base'.[57] And there is an understanding that good fortune and bad fortune ebb and flow naturally. As one anonymous collection of folk wisdom advises: 'Grief seems to be the sister of joy', or, as the moral states, 'a fine day must necessarily be followed by a storm'.[58] A belief in luck was a way of dealing better with this seemingly inevitable cycle of boom and bust. A belief in random chance would offer nothing but hopelessness and despair whereas luck could be managed to produce a better outcome. In the fable of the fishermen and tunny-fish, some fishermen put out to fish and, after struggling for a long time without catching a thing, were sitting dejectedly in their boat. At that point a tunny happened to leap into the boat. As the moral states, 'so it is that chance often bestows what skill cannot provide'.[59] To see this as the deliberate favouring of luck reflects a worldview which understands the relationship between man and nature as being regulated by the gods. It turns the arbitrary and irregular into the intentional and purposeful. It is a view that the reality of having to earn a living from an uncertain and dangerous environment itself helped generate.

This outlook also reflected a belief that the world did not lie entirely at the mercy of fate. Luck was reified as something that could enable its possessors to improve their chances of survival in the risky world they inhabited. This reflected a more optimistic view of the world, as a place that could be transformed by the actions of men. It was not simply man's

---

[56] M. Beck and B. Kewell, *Risk: A Study of Its Origins, History and Politics*, New Jersey: World Scientific, 2014, pp. 20–1.
[57] Artemidorus, *The Interpretation of Dreams* 2.37.
[58] Anon., *Collectio Augustana*, in Hansen, *Anthology of Ancient Greek Popular Literature*, pp. 265–6.
[59] Aesop, *Fable* 21.

A Belief in Luck

lot to accept his fate with resignation. But the unpredictability of divine favour meant that mortals could never be sure or even confident of divine support. Constant acts of devotion were therefore necessary to encourage the gods to maintain their support and influence the outcome. Luck was also, in some sense, predetermined. As the saying went, 'the unfortunate cannot escape their misfortune'.[60] Luck would come in its own good time, and the carrying out of proper ritual devotion and customary practices was simply the necessary precondition for it to come at all. As a consequence, high-risk activities such as sailing became dominated by various rituals designed to win over the gods. According to one tradition, nobody on board a ship was allowed to cut their hair or nails except during a terrible storm.[61] It was considered bad luck to leave port on 24 August, 5 October or 8 November. Sneezing during embarkation foretold doom, as did seeing a crow or magpie in the rigging. To dream of goats was bad, of owls meant storms or pirates, and of gulls signalled danger but not death. This did not reflect mere superstition. For fishermen, for example, life consisted in an endless repetition of the dangerous cycle of putting out to sea, fishing and returning with whatever luck had granted them. It was a world where little changed, and so it made sense to try to win over the gods in a formulaic, repetitive way. It seemed sensible to adhere to what had worked before and to reproduce what had been effective in the past, however limited that effect might seem.

It was understood that there were limits to the degree to which the gods could be influenced. In one fable, a sudden storm threatened to sink a ship. One of the voyagers tore his clothes and called on the gods with great weeping and wailing, promising to make offerings if he was spared. When the storm died down again and the sea was calm, those on board danced and jumped for joy at having so unexpectedly escaped. But the helmsman said to them, 'our rejoicing ought to be regulated by the fact that we will have another storm if our luck runs that way'. As the moral stated, the fable 'teaches us not to be too elated at good fortune since we know the fickleness of fortune'.[62]

Risk was an unavoidable part of life, but in response to that a culture developed that used beliefs and practices to mitigate the impact. Luck was personified and seen as something that could be managed and possessed.

---

[60] Heliodorus, *The Aethiopian Story* 5.19.
[61] Juvenal, *Satire* 12.81; Petronius, *Satyricon* 103–4. See L. Casson, *Travel in the Ancient World*, London: Allen & Unwin, 1974, pp. 149–62, 'On the sea'.
[62] Aesop, *Fable* 78.

Rather than being overwhelmed by the size of the threats they faced, relying on the good will of the gods effectively insulated people from this sensation.[63] But belief in luck also implied an acceptance that the gods ultimately dictated the path of future events. The ability of humanity to affect its future was limited and to try to change anything fundamental about how society was ordered was futile. Vulnerability was simply an aspect of the human condition. All that could be done was to try and drive bad luck away on to some other poor soul, a permanent battle of beggar-thy-neighbour tactics. A limited good, to be sure, but it did offer some cause for hope.

A Belief in Risk-Taking

All societies designate certain risks as being unacceptable and worth avoiding.[64] But societies also valorise certain risks as being worth undertaking because of the benefits they are perceived to bring if a successful outcome is achieved. As we have seen, the modern term 'risk' emerged from maritime trade and the high levels of both danger and return that this involved. Societies allow and expect individuals to take certain gambles with their personal lives if they are to improve their situation. Modern financial theory highlights how risk can also generate returns.[65] Investors require a higher level of expected return to entice them to invest in higher-risk assets. Modernity has also seen an increase in risky sports where the adrenalin rush produced by putting oneself in danger is perceived to make the risk worth taking.

Risk-avoidance with the aim of staying safe was certainly not perceived as an automatic good in the Roman world. Beard has argued that Romans engaged in what she calls an 'aleatory society', emphasising that such engagement in risk-taking behaviour was active. Caesar metaphorically threw the dice when he crossed the Rubicon in defiance of the Senate and the law. It was a high-risk strategy that could have ended in defeat and death.[66] Caesar's appetite for risk was by no means abnormal for an upper-class man. Polybius' work contains a description of an aristocratic Roman funeral which shows how much pressure elite families placed on their

---

[63] For an interesting analysis of the role of luck in a modern setting, see J. Zulaika, *Terranova: The Ethos and Luck of Deep-Sea Fishermen*, Philadelphia: Institute for the Study of Human Issues, 1981, esp. ch. 3, 'The order of luck', pp. 65–94.

[64] See J. O. Zinn (ed.), *Social Theories of Risk and Uncertainty: An Introduction*, Oxford: Blackwell, 2008.

[65] See Markowitz, 'Portfolio selection'.   [66] Beard, 'Risk and the humanities; alea iacta est'.

young men to undertake high levels of personal risk for the sake of the wider family's reputational and financial benefit.[67] The corpse was carried to the rostra in the Roman Forum, where it was usually stood upright, and the deceased's son would then deliver a eulogy outlining his father's achievements. The procession would include actors wearing the face masks of ancestors in order to recreate accurately the appearance of dead family members. The actors were chosen because they were the same height or size as the dead, and they would recreate any particular mannerisms the ancestors had possessed. They would dress in clothes according to rank, so, if the ancestor was a consul, he wore a toga with purple stripes, if a censor, a toga of pure purple, or, if he had also celebrated a triumph for his military successes, then a toga embroidered with gold. These representatives of the dead rode in chariots, carrying the insignia of the offices they had held, and led the procession according to their rank. Polybius notes that there could not be a more inspiring spectacle for an ambitious young nobleman than to see the collected glory of his family brought alive before him. The speaker would outline each ancestor's achievements. The message was clear: young aristocratic men were expected to undergo significant personal risk for familial and communal benefits and pursue high public office and military success above all else. As confirmation of the inspirational effect of this ceremony, Polybius notes that many Romans deliberately accepted near-certain death for the benefit of Rome.

Obviously this kind of ceremony happened only among the most blue-blooded families. But we can see this as acting as an inspiration across society, and Polybius notes that the public nature of the funeral and procession was designed to be seen by the general populace. Nor are his examples of bravery confined to the elite. We can also find plenty of examples of risk-adopting behaviour among the lower levels of Roman society. Gladiators and charioteers, for example, generally came from the ranks of slaves, yet they could become celebrities on account of the high level of personal risk they were compelled to run in order to entertain the Roman populace. Benefiting the people in this way could, for the most successful, bring with it not just fame but substantial financial rewards. Perhaps the most successful charioteer of all time, Diocles, who raced in the second century CE over a period of twenty-four years, won prize money totalling 35,863,120 sesterces.[68] He competed in 4,257 races, meaning that each time he risked his life by racing he earned an average of 8,425 sesterces, almost ten times what a legionary earned in a year. Diocles was

[67] Polybius, *Histories* 6.53–4. [68] *CIL* 6.10048 and 14.2884.

obviously exceptional, but as a symbol of the upward economic mobility that even a slave (such as he probably was initially) could attain he was significant, just as the lowering of legal status (*infamia*) he automatically suffered by being a charioteer reflected how limited was his upward social mobility.

It would be wrong to see this attitude as extending equally across all strata of Roman society. Most Roman notions of risk-taking seem to have been highly gendered, with men taking the risks that women could only observe. Attitudes to risk were also affected by other sociological factors, such as status and age. To a large extent this reflected the vulnerability of the risk-taker to volatility in income. Those with deep pockets were more likely to have a higher appetite for ventures with a substantial range of possible outcomes. Put simply, the difference between success and failure was often extreme. Caesar's conquest of Gaul repaid the money he had borrowed to fund his earlier political career and paid for his legions that carried out the conquest. Failure would have finished him. Similarly, the wealthy were able to invest in potentially highly lucrative ventures such as shipping even though the returns depended entirely upon the safe arrival of the ships. At the other end of the social scale, those living close to subsistence level were much more vulnerable to volatility because they lacked the savings and other resources to cope with losses. Instead, they concentrated on managing their possible downside risks, even if the cost of doing so was to forfeit some upside potential.

Broadly speaking, therefore, risk tolerance was inversely related to social status. Beard's aleatory society may largely have been the society of the upper classes. It was those with power who were least likely to perceive the world as a place full of dangers rather than opportunities. But we should remember that Diocles almost certainly started his career as a charioteer as a slave. The decision to risk his life was made by an owner whose asset he was, but he clearly embraced that decision. Being at the bottom of society may well have encouraged risk-taking. Interestingly, Tacitus notes that both the utterly poor and the vastly rich could be shamelessly reckless. In fact, recklessness was associated with the needy.[69] Perhaps by the time individuals sank into destitution their risk appetite increased, since they had nothing more to lose. What the Romans in the middle felt is hard to ascertain. The nouveau riche freedman Trimalchio is portrayed by Petronius in the *Satyricon* as displaying a reckless attitude to speculation in shipping and trading, where his fortunes oscillate to the tune of tens of

---

[69] Tacitus, *Annals* 3.54.

millions of sesterces per day. Trimalchio is a caricature of the ambitious freedman, aspiring to move up the social ladder by copying the risk-taking attitudes of the elite to an absurd degree. But this description represents the sneering attitude of a wealthy elite writer and we should not see it as evidence of widespread risk appetite.

Gambling

A more realistic idea of popular attitudes to risk can be found in the widespread activity of gambling, which was enjoyed by people across the social spectrum.[70] Its popularity reflected the major part that chance played in everyday life and we can interpret Roman gambling as expressing their culture's most important features in a concentrated form. Play and leisure activities often copy elements of the serious world in which they occur, as Geertz showed in his analysis of the Balinese cockfight. Yet it is also the case that the Romans had no conscious understanding of the probabilities involved in the games they played. They indulged in a kind of pragmatic thinking about uncertainty that was probabilistic but nothing more precise than that. We can also see it as an analogy for how the Romans dealt with risk in their wider lives, providing an education for its participants in the various life skills that would enable them to survive in a world of substantial uncertainty.

Gambling trained its participants in the skills of numerical calculation, albeit of a limited kind, and expressed the necessity of being able to carry out risk assessment in daily life. In a world where incomes were vulnerable, the average Roman needed to learn when to be cautious and risk-averse and when to risk more. The tactical nous demanded by the board game reflected the kind of cunning that helped individuals secure the resources they needed.[71] As Purcell has noted, these games involved 'numerical sophistication', and invite us to see numeracy as being a valued part of non-elite life.[72] Being quick with numbers and fractions acted as a kind of ancient technological advantage.[73] Gambling required the individual to

---

[70] On gambling see J. Toner, *Leisure and Ancient Rome*, Cambridge: Polity, 1995, pp. 89–101; and 'The intellectual life of the Roman non-elite', in L. Grig (ed.), *Popular Culture in the Ancient World*, Cambridge: Cambridge University Press, 2016, pp. 167–88; N. Purcell, 'Literate games: Roman urban society and the game of alea', *Past & Present*, 147 (1995), 3–37.

[71] See, for example, Polybius, *Histories* 1.84.7–8; Ovid, *Art of Love* 3.355–60.

[72] Purcell, 'Literate games', p. 4.

[73] See the appendix on interest rate calculations in N. Horsfall, *The Culture of the Roman Plebs*, London: Duckworth, 2003, pp. 17–19.

make calculated decisions under pressure, and to deal with the volatility of returns that winning or losing brought. Gambling and board games also required the learning of a significant body of detailed knowledge, paralleling the kind of niche expertise which could enhance income, either through learning a trade or through skill as a farmer. Gambling was seen in part as a technical skill, as, for example, in Claudius' treatise on gambling.[74] It is striking that one of the brags inscribed on a surviving gaming board is: 'You don't know how to play (*ludere nescis*).' Knowledge was what marked out the good gambler from the bad. It also enabled the player to assess opponents' tactics and to spot cheating, and indeed to carry it out.

Gambling taught important social lessons, too. It showed how skill could be used to enhance reputation, with those playing well gaining prestige for doing so: Piso was 'so good and clever in the game of little soldiers that people would gather round him as he played'.[75] Gambling opened up for the successful participant an avenue for improving his or her financial position and thereby status in society. In reality, of course, we can imagine that most gambling was for small stakes that would never have any concrete effect on status. And we know that probabilities would even out in the long term, meaning that games of chance would not produce any real social mobility. But for the Romans, who did not understand that luck would largely even out, gambling encapsulated their life of small social gains and losses and expressed a desire to achieve social advancement. The use of money served to underline that something important was literally at stake. By contrast, when Claudius is punished in the afterlife in Seneca's *Apocolocyntosis*, it is by being condemned to gamble endlessly and pointlessly. It was not the taking part that mattered, it was the winning.

Gambling highlighted that most risks arose in a local communal setting. Surrounded by competitive peers, Roman men and women were expected to be able to hold their own. This aggressive society was reflected in the abusive counters that were used, bearing such taunts as 'drunkard' and 'adulterer'. Cheating was all part of this kind of behaviour. But the form that Roman gambling took also reflected a strong social side to this competitiveness. The local group also created a sense of camaraderie: Ammianus noted that in Rome, 'where all friendships are rather cool', it was only those friendships created between gamblers which were sociable and intimate.[76] They had been forged in the heat of the gaming

---

[74] Purcell, 'Literate games', p. 30.   [75] [Probus], *Note on Juvenal's Satire* 5.109.
[76] Ammianus Marcellinus 28.4.21.

community. In this regard, the counters did not only reflect simple abuse, they also acted as symbols of the competitive banter that served to glue together these local communities.

Gambling was, it should be noted, also stigmatised in certain ways. It was illegal except on certain festival days and when games were played for small stakes after dinner. And a literary trope is of the rich son who loses his fortune at the gaming board. Gambling was also seen as almost synonymous with violence, and the laws make reference to the fights that gambling seemed habitually to generate as do various representations of gamblers in mosaics and tavern wall-paintings.[77] What these highlight is that taking unnecessary or excessive risks was seen as potentially destabilising, both for the individual who might lose his or her social status by losing large sums and societally because gambling was seen as promoting dispute and conflict. The story of how Augustus gambled with extreme moderation relies on such concerns.[78] The emperor is perfectly happy to have a reputation for regular gambling but always made sure that he did so in a controlled, and indeed controlling, way. The stakes were relatively small, considering that his wealth could have afforded colossal sums, and the emperor went so far as to provide his playing partners with their own stake money, which he then generously allowed them to win and retain. We can interpret the image as a metaphor for how he wanted his rule to be seen: a world where the emperor made the world safe and beneficial by controlling the risks everyone faced.

Gambling can also be interpreted as another expression of a belief in luck: however much life was affected by chance, individuals were not entirely at the mercy of fate. The supernatural could be encouraged to show favour by means of, for example, spells: 'let not even one of these playing with me be equal, and I am going to throw what I want'.[79] Modern observations of gambling note that many players employ strategies that they believe will help them to 'beat the system'.[80] There is no surviving evidence for whether Roman gamblers shared this outlook, but it seems plausible that a belief in their ability to encourage divine support reflects a parallel view of the individual as having some agency even in a world dominated by chance.

---

[77] See *Digest* 11.5 for various laws relating to gambling-related violence. Wall paintings from the Caupona of Salvius in Pompeii also depict men fighting about the outcome of gaming.
[78] Suetonius, *Augustus* 71.
[79] *PGM* 7.423–8, in Betz, H. D. (ed.), *The Greek Magical Papyri in Translation, Including the Demotic Spells*, Chicago: University of Chicago Press, 1992.
[80] I. K. Zola, 'Observations on gambling in a lower-class setting', *Social Problems*, 10 (1963), 353–61.

Gambling in the modern world can be theorised as representing an escape from the dull routines of a world where most risks have been eradicated or strictly limited. Gambling in this view is a form of 'edgework', a high-risk leisure activity undertaken voluntarily by the participants.[81] Modernity has seen an upsurge in interest in various extreme sports that place the individual in a situation where the usual risk controls do not seem to apply and the resulting adrenalin rush is seen as providing a powerful means of self-actualisation. It is hard to see Roman gambling as displaying a comparable attitude to risk, for the simple fact that ancient life was in no way derisked. But we can detect a similarly positive attitude to exposing the self to potential harm. As Beard puts it, 'Rome was a culture that looked danger in the eye'.[82] Roman culture did not attempt to remove risks but rather celebrated the opportunities that uncertainty could bring. It used the imagery of dicing to express the sense that belief and the luck of the board game became a way of understanding what in our terms would be thought of as risk.[83]

Risk and Identity

Rome's risk culture encouraged certain personality traits in its members. We have seen how elite males were pressured by their families to embrace ambitious risk-taking and how making a living in a dangerous environment helped generate a belief in luck. We can see a similar social force being exerted in gambling, which encouraged individuals of all statuses to act in public in a competitive and quick-witted manner. Attitudes to risk were therefore central to the construction of identity.

We can see this kind of pressure reflected in the well-known saying, 'Fortune favours the brave' (*Fortuna fortibus favet*). From the human standpoint, this provided another means to influence the decisions of the deity: display the correct attitude and you are more likely to win divine support. But from a societal point of view, it can be interpreted as encouraging a risk-taking mentality. It is no surprise to find that the temple dedicated to Fortuna Huiusce Diei (Fortune of This Day, meaning something like the Luck of the Moment), which stood in the Area Sacra di Largo Argentina in Rome, had been promised by the general Lutatius Catulus immediately before the battle of Vercellae in 101 BCE, when he faced the attack of the Cimbri, who were so numerous that they resembled

---

[81] S. Lyng (ed.), *Edgework: The Sociology of Risk Taking*, London: Routledge, 2005.
[82] Beard, 'Risk and the humanities; alea iacta est', p. 98.   [83] Ibid., p. 92.

a 'vast sea in motion'.[84] Similarly, the temple of Fortuna Equestris (Fortune of the Equestrians), located near to the Theatre of Pompey, was built by Fulvius Flaccus in fulfilment of a vow made to the goddess during his campaign against the Celtiberians in Spain in 180 BCE.[85] The final battle was, Livy tells us, a 'desperate one, with changing fortune (varia fortuna)'. When the Celts adopted a wedge formation, the Roman line was all but broken and Fulvius shouted to his cavalry that the army was lost unless they came to the rescue. This they duly did, disintegrating the wedge with their courageous charges and turning the enemy to flight. Watching them flee, the Roman commander promised a temple to this equine aspect of Fortuna.

That the various classes of Roman society could be expected to display such bravery in different ways was also reflected in other sides of the goddess. Fortuna could be both Patrician or Plebeian, as well as Equestrian, perhaps reflecting the various roles chance played on the battlefield. Fortuna was a widely worshipped goddess and a wide variety of titles were used to describe the many ways in which she impacted upon life. She could be *Primigenia* in that she determined whether a family's first-born child would live to perpetuate its name. She could be *Publica* in her role as tutelary goddess of the state. As protector of the emperor, she could be *Augusta*; as guardian of the household, she could be *Privata*. Fortuna represented a divine power that seemed to pervade all areas of ancient life, an influence that needed to be understood in widely diverse forms that itself reflected an understanding that the breadth of the goddess' impact required a great variety of human responses.

Attitudes towards dealing with Fortuna expressed attitudes towards taking risk. These helped to establish moral habits such as prudence and patience. If we look at the dice-oracle pillar from Kremna in central Pisidia, we find in the answers that choosing the right time to act becomes all important. It was crucial not to act intemperately. As is stated by throw ten, called 'the throw of Fortune the Helmsman', this was no time for frivolous enthusiasm, which will do 'great harm'. Or as throw twenty-two puts it, 'stay calm, for the time is not yet ripe. If you make frivolous haste in vain, you will pursue a goal that is out of reach. I do not yet see the right moment, but if you relax a little, you will achieve success'. Success also meant accepting that you could not always get the gods to favour you: 'It is not profitable for you to force the gods inopportunely' (fourteen). But the inference is clear that there will be times when divine power can be won

---

[84] Plutarch, *Life of Marius* 26.   [85] Livy 40.40 and 44.

over and success attained. As throw seven, Of Victory, states: 'You will win, you will take what you wish, and everything will be yours.' Not only that, but the gods themselves will respect you: 'The Daimon treats you as worthy of honour and you will overcome your enemies.'

Roman personality types were in this way suited to dealing with the risks they faced in life. It is possible to see the different types of gladiators as corresponding to these various personality types. The solid, active, hard worker at one end of the spectrum, personified by the heavily armed *secutor*, stood against the quick-witted trickster in the form of the net fighter, the *retiarius*. This dubious aspect of the *retiarius* made him the most reprehensible type, even among the shameful class of gladiators as a whole. He wore no mask, which would otherwise cover his shame from appearing in public, was almost naked, and he carried inferior weapons. A trident and net were fit for a lowly fisherman not a soldier. We also find a symbolic equivalence between personality type and different gladiators in ancient dream interpretation. Artemidorus explains that to dream of fighting as a gladiator signified marriage, with the opponent in the dream indicating what character of woman the wife will be. 'For example', he says, 'if a man fights a Thracian, he will marry a wife who is rich, crafty, and fond of being first.' She will be crafty, because the Thracian's sword is not straight. But to dream of a *retiarius* signified a poor and wanton wife, 'a woman who roams about consorting very freely with anyone who wants her'.[86]

The reply of Secundus, the Silent Philosopher, to the question 'what is a sailor?' drew an equivalence between the characteristics needed by those making a living at sea and those in the arena. A sailor was 'the opponent of the storm', who is 'unsure of his safety', and 'a neighbour to death', and, in a phrase which neatly encapsulates all the dangers and constant risk assessments that struggling with the sea entailed, he was 'a marine gladiator'.[87] Both characters had to cope with high levels of uncertainty, where controlled aggression probably helped in self-preservation. One of the reasons for the popularity of gladiators may have been that they reflected the kinds of Roman personality types that spectators recognised in their daily lives. They also served as an inspiration in the same way that the ancestors of the elite did at funerals. Equally, the fact that the sea generated so many dangerous situations made it 'good to think with', and many Roman fables use it to exemplify making difficult decisions. In the fable of

---

[86] Artemidorus, *The Interpretation of Dreams* 2.32.
[87] See Hansen, *Anthology of Ancient Greek Popular Literature*, p. 73.

the coot, the bat and the bramble's shipping business, the venture ends in disaster. They lose everything, the coot is inconsolable and 'since then the coot has been diving down to the bottom, looking for her bronze'.[88] The message is clear that not only should you diversify and not risk everything in one go, but you also have to be resilient in the face of disaster. Danger was an inevitable part of ancient life and being tough was an important attribute for the individual to possess.

Conclusion

Living against a backdrop of constant dangers, in combination with certain cultural predispositions, helped to create a cultural system. Various risk management strategies enabled the Romans to cope better, ranging from diversification to patronage and managing social relations. This all required calculation: deciding which children to feed if food ran short; planning for potential threats to particular crops; spreading losses when they did occur in a way that the family unit would best survive as a going concern; slowly managing to get back to normality after a shock. But this calculation was not of a numerical type and relied largely on the received wisdom of the past, even though this could be interpreted according to current needs. Risk-aversion was probably just as important as risk-taking. The poor, in particular, found in fables much advice to steer clear of men more powerful than themselves or to avoid getting tangled up in any kind of legal dispute. But the Romans also understood the benefits of embracing risk in order to improve their status in society.

What we would see as random throws of the dice were in the Roman world imbued with meaning. Chance was conceptualised as a divine power that could itself be influenced, thereby leaving the door open for some individual agency and purpose. Risk may have been an inherent part of ordinary life, but a culture developed in response that used beliefs and practices to soften its impact. These practices served as metacommentaries that taught the Romans what they needed to know in order to survive in this risky environment and encouraged them to develop particular personality traits that were thought to enable them to display resilience in the face of inevitable danger.

[88] Aesop, *Fable* 171.

CHAPTER 4

Risk Management

I have argued so far that risk should be seen as an active concept that involves a certain level of calculation about the future, albeit not necessarily of a numerical kind. Chapter 3 looked at a range of methods the Romans employed to help plan for the future, which involved a lesser degree of conscious calculation since they relied heavily on the knowledge that had been handed down the generations: what I termed a 'risk culture'. This chapter examines areas of knowledge where the Romans displayed expertise and consciously sought to develop techniques and systems that enabled them to better understand and control future uncertainties. I begin by looking at architecture, military logistics and law, before moving on to aspects of financial management, such as maritime loans, interest rates, and annuities. I then finish by looking at the probabilistic thinking involved in the religious practices of oracle and dream interpretation.

What is immediately apparent is that the ancients did not rely solely on religion to deal with uncertainty. The Romans thought systematically and creatively about many areas where future uncertainty could be assessed and managed. These approaches were not statistical but all show an awareness of a range of likelihoods and possibilities. Bernstein has argued that, 'without numbers, risk is wholly a matter of gut', but Roman expertise shows that this is not the case.[1] The Romans did not have statistical models, nor had they worked out how to calculate probabilities, but they did develop a range of sophisticated ways of dealing with the many unknowns they faced.

Architecture

Rome is famous for its buildings. From the Colosseum to the Pantheon, the Romans used their architectural skills to construct huge numbers of

---

[1] Bernstein, *Against the Gods*, p. 23.

inspirational and long-lasting edifices. Clearly this was not a question of luck. Roman architects lacked sophisticated mathematical methods to calculate the physical laws of structure, but they were able to extrapolate by means of observation and experience. It is apparent that they understood one of the most fundamental rules of structural design: 'that gravitational loadings increase with the cube, and cross sections with the square, of a structure's linear scale'.[2] While this sounds complicated in theory, in practice it was easily understandable because the volume of building material required increased exponentially according to size. The corollary to this rule was that gravitationally induced stresses increased at an exponential rate as a building grew bigger. Roman builders also 'intuited, on some level, the principle of structural redundancy, or *statical indeterminacy*', whereby all buildings are in equilibrium and bear their load by means of a complex and invisible mesh of stress lines. The Romans therefore built in a manner that included structural margins of error that created various paths for each force. Sometimes they realised that certain supporting elements could be removed, and the widespread use of the oculus, most famously in the Pantheon, shows that builders understood the principle of the compression ring. None of this was done with any theoretical understanding but was based on a combination of experience and an intuition that was inculcated by careful observation.[3] Not surprisingly, the slow accretion of expertise meant that knowledge was sometimes handed down through the generations and building families, such as the Haterii, came to be involved in the construction of several imperial building projects over long periods of time.

A variety of preparatory methods were used to help design buildings, including drawings, scale models and sketches.[4] Vitruvius describes the use of measured drawings. The first represented the ground plan, drawn by ruler and compass. The second showed the front elevation. The third, a perspective drawing, drew the front and the receding sides to their vanishing points.[5] Similarly, he understood the ratios that should be

---

[2] R. Taylor, *Roman Builders: A Study in Architectural Process*, Cambridge: Cambridge University Press, 2003, p. 48.
[3] Ibid. pp. 49–55.
[4] Vitruvius, *On Architecture* 1.2.2; 3.5.8. See J. P. Oleson (ed.), *The Oxford Handbook of Engineering and Technology in the Classical World*, Oxford: Oxford University Press, 2008, esp. L. Lancaster, 'Roman engineering and construction', pp. 256–85.
[5] This does not mean that Roman architects used the kind of infinite single-point perspective developed during the Renaissance. Rather, it has been described as an image set in 'conventional perspectives of a cartographical type'. See W. Dorigo, *Late Roman Painting: A Study of Pictorial Records, 30 BC–AD 500*, trans. J. Cleugh and J. Warrington, London: Dent, 1971, p. 73.

employed in the use of columns to dictate the proportionate size of the architrave. In the case of the Pantheon, the builders recognised that the lateral thrusts of the ceiling needed to be controlled by using lighter concrete at the top and buttressing on the outside of the cylinder building. Roman designers also realised that large buildings on weak ground needed substantial foundations, such as the ring of concrete that served as the base for the Colosseum, which is seven metres thick in places.

Elsewhere, deep foundations were used to counteract the risk of an earthquake. The temple of Jupiter at Baalbek has foundations up to seventeen metres deep. This indicates that the locals were well aware of the dangers that they were exposing themselves to by inhabiting such an area and that they took active steps to reduce the threat. But it is also clear that it was considered worth taking such precautions only for the most high-value projects. By contrast, when certain small towns were struck by an earthquake, few buildings would survive. The city of Baelo Claudia, in southern Spain, experienced two major quakes, occurring sometime between 40–60 and 350–95 CE. The ruins reveal collapsed columns, distorted buildings and the collapse of house and city walls, as well as the warping of street pavements. After the second destruction, the inhabitants decided to abandon the site and simply left.[6]

A strange story from late in the empire shows that Roman builders understood something of the structural stresses created by an earthquake. An engineer called Anthemius had fallen out with his neighbour Zeno, who lived above him, and wanted to get his revenge. Anthemius filled some huge cauldrons with water and covered them with tapering, trumpet-like pipes. He then fixed the upper ends of these pipes to the beams and joists of the ceiling. With this apparatus in place, he lit fires beneath these great cauldrons and as the water boiled the steam it produced travelled up the pipes and exerted pressure on the woodwork. Little by little the pressure increased until it became so great that it shook the whole structure. Yet as an engineer, the historian Agathias informs us, Anthemius had been careful not to overdo it, given that any collapse would have seen him lose his home too. Instead he calculated that the steam would exert just enough force to make the woodwork creak and wobble slightly. Fearing the onset of an earthquake, a terrified Zeno ran for his life.[7] The story probably tells us as much about the degree to which Roman buildings

---

[6] P. G. Silva et al., 'Archaeoseismic record at the ancient Roman city of Baelo Claudia (Cádiz, south Spain)', *Tectonophysics*, 408 (2005), 129–46.
[7] The story is set in late antique Constantinople in Agathias, *Histories* 5.7.

incorporated significant margins of error as the engineer's ability to calculate the forces accurately. But it does suggest that engineers were expected to know about such matters, even if such knowledge resulted almost entirely from experience rather than theory.

And, of course, we have ample evidence that many Roman buildings did not exhibit such resilience. Collapse seems to have been commonplace. The third man of the first Triumvirate with Caesar and Pompey, Crassus, famously made his fortune by buying up property in Rome on the cheap from distressed sellers. He had noticed how often Rome was hit by fires and how people died and *insulae* collapsed as a result, 'owing to their being too massive and close together', which suggests that Roman architects were perfectly capable of making errors of judgement.[8] Even if we see such collapse as being caused by the fire and not a reflection on Roman building techniques, other evidence underlines the instability of much Roman housing. Juvenal describes how Rome was a city of tottering houses supported by props, where patches covered gaping cracks in the walls, and the inhabitants slept under roofs that could collapse at any moment.[9] This is perhaps satirical excess, but Cicero earlier had casually written about how two of his shops had fallen down, while the rest were cracking so badly that even the mice had fled.[10] He takes this entirely in his stride, as if it were normal, while displaying no concern for his tenants, and determines to rebuild in a profitable way. The Greek geographical writer Strabo similarly remarks how urban building activity is constantly aimed at replacing structures lost to collapse and fire.[11] Archaeology can also provide ample evidence of dodgy Roman building techniques, with inadequate foundations, mortar mixtures containing insufficient lime and improperly baked bricks that dissolved in the rain. The walls of some *insulae* in Pompeii reveal that the inner core, which should have consisted of a solid mix of mortar and aggregate, was in reality a mix of rubble and clay that would have been highly susceptible to water damage.[12]

What such evidence emphasises is that Roman building techniques generally reflected the budget behind the project. Larger-scale, imperially backed builds were more likely to last because contractors were unlikely to try to cut corners or use cheap materials. It is noteworthy that the collapse of the wooden amphitheatre at the town of Fidenae resulted after a local

---

[8] Plutarch, *Crassus* 2.4.   [9] Juvenal, *Satire* 3.190–204.   [10] Cicero, *Letters to Atticus* 14.9.
[11] Strabo, *Geography* 5.3.235.
[12] G. S. Aldrete, *Floods of the Tiber in Ancient Rome*, Baltimore, MD: Johns Hopkins University Press, 2007, pp. 109–10.

businessman called Atilius erected the arena to host a gladiatorial show.[13] Looking for a quick profit, he had failed either to lay the foundations in solid ground or to secure the fastenings of the wooden structure above. The show was a sell-out, with interest fanned by the emperor Tiberius' recent ban on gladiatorial shows, and over 50,000 crowded into the flimsy structure. Unable to cope with the weight of so many, it collapsed. Such large, high-profile architectural failures seem to have been rare. We can see this perhaps most clearly in Caligula's supposed belief that the Fidenae collapse was the most famous event during Tiberius' reign and that perversely he wished for a comparable disaster to mark his own rule.[14] The reclusive Tiberius had himself felt obliged to leave his island retreat at Capri in order to visit the scene.[15] The Senate's response, which decreed that in the future only those eligible for the equestrian class should be allowed to put on games and that all amphitheatres should have solid foundations, displayed an awareness of both building technique and status. It was understood that large structures needed solid foundations but also that only the upper classes could be relied upon to maintain standards and not give in to greed. That Atilius himself escaped with being exiled also suggests that no great fault was attributed to him, perhaps because the authorities had no way of assessing the degree to which the collapse was the result of his shoddy building or the result of the behaviour of the crowd.

Imperial responses to building collapse came as part of a parcel of organisational reforms that reveal an understanding of the principal risks posed by such constructions. Augustus, for example, set up the Nightwatch (*vigiles*) to help fight fires at the same time as he established a limit of seventy feet for the height of new and existing buildings.[16] Both factors were probably linked in the imperial mind because the one easily caused the other. Fire led to building collapse, building collapse easily resulted in fire from the lethal presence of both wood and the oil in the lamps used for lighting. Other imperial reorganisations tried to manage and control the flood risks faced by the city and its people. The constant danger posed by flooding of the river Tiber demanded a concerted effort to manage the flow of water into the main channel and to clear the main channel itself. Julius Caesar planned to divert the river, which was probably linked to the expansion of the city into the Campus Martius. Augustus responded by attempting to limit the human impact on the flow of the Tiber. He cleared the riverbed of any rubbish dumped in it and

---

[13] Tacitus, *Annals* 4.62–3. [14] Suetonius, *Caligula* 31. [15] Suetonius, *Tiberius* 40.
[16] Strabo, *Geography* 5.3.235.

removed buildings away from the banks while widening the river's channel.[17] This was done not just to prevent flooding but to help shipping. Tiberius tried to control the water flow after heavy flooding in 12 and 15 CE, and it is interesting to note that two courses of action were decided upon.[18] The first was to consult the Sibylline Books. The second was to commission a survey of what was physically feasible. The consultation of the books shows how any natural disaster was seen as representing some form of divine displeasure and so required a religious response. But that did not prevent more technical actions designed to mitigate the flow of the river in the future. The report proposed that two upstream tributaries should be diverted and that flood plains should be established.

The reasons for the eventual rejection of the plan are also revealing. Complaints from affected cities highlighted the economic cost of losing fertile agricultural land but it was also feared that the plan risked offending the river god of the Tiber. Imperial responses therefore show how future danger was recognised, both in terms of an environmental hazard which posed a direct threat to the city and in terms of how human actions could exacerbate this risk, but also how this understanding was limited and set within a religious framework that could dictate what, if any, action should be taken.[19] It is also noticeable that larger-scale environmental hazards were treated by religious means, since any remedial action required a higher level of technical knowledge than the Romans possessed, and that uncertainty was reflected in a lack of confidence about the potential impact on the divine. Imperial action was focused on redressing the smaller-scale human activities that were adversely affecting the river.

What is also evident from this, is that the Romans understood that they inhabited a dangerous environment but accepted this because of the concomitant benefits. Pliny the Elder neatly encapsulated the reason why the Romans bore the risks associated with the Tiber when he described it as 'their blessing and their curse'. The river's usual calm flow meant that large ships were able to navigate its waters and import goods from overseas, but when the floods came it left large numbers of inhabitants exposed to

---

[17] Suetonius, *Augustus* 30. [18] Tacitus, *Annals* 1.76, 79
[19] See M. Ronin, 'The perception of natural risks of earthquakes and floods in the Roman world', *Historia*, 71 (2022), 362–89. On the use of rites of expiation, construction techniques and pieces of imperial legislation to manage risks, see P. Deeg, *Der Kaiser und die Katastrophe: Untersuchungen zum politischen Umgang mit Umweltkatastrophen im Prinzipat (31 v. Chr. bis 192 n. Chr.)*, Stuttgart: Franz Steiner, 2019, pp. 204–10; cf. H. Sonnabend, *Naturkatastrophen in der Antike: Wahrnehmung, Deutung, Management*, Stuttgart: J. B. Metzler, 1999, p. 242.

the dangers of flooding.[20] Augustus also understood that the management of this risk needed to be upgraded *pari passu* with the expansion of the city. Abandoning the earlier reliance on elected officials, he established permanent boards of appointees; these included citizens of all classes so that all Roman residents had a stake in controlling the risk posed by the environment.[21] Similarly, the city itself was divided by him into fourteen municipal districts in 7 BCE, which represented an effort to improve both the quality of the urban administration and its status. High-quality, large-scale urban planning in areas such as engineering, water control and construction now came to be seen as peculiarly Roman skills, or, as Strabo puts it, 'the Romans had the best foresight in those matters which the Greeks thought little of, such as the construction of roads and aqueducts, and of sewers that could wash out the filth of the city into the Tiber'.[22]

Logistics

We also find a variety of attempts at governmental planning in areas such as the underwriting of the risks involved in the transportation and supply of goods. This is particularly the case with military logistics. It should come as little surprise to discover that the Roman military machine demanded careful planning to keep it on the march, all of which involved the assessment of future threats and taking steps to avoid or mitigate the impact of these dangers. As the military writer Vegetius spells out: 'Whoever does not provide for provisions and other necessities is conquered without fighting.'[23]

The term 'logistics' has two component parts. The first is the calculation of the assets needed in war. The second refers to the supply, transport, storage and organisation of these assets.[24] These military needs can be substantial in quantity and cover a wide variety of materials, including clothing, weaponry, animals, vehicles, tools, firewood and construction materials. An army marches on its stomach, and the Roman military was no different, requiring supplies of meat (generally pork and lamb), pulses,

---

[20] See Ronin, 'The perception of natural risks'. [21] Suetonius, *Augustus* 30.
[22] Strabo, *Geography* 5.3.235, after Loeb translation.
[23] Vegetius, *Epitome of Military Matters* 3.26; on provisioning, 3.1–3; cf. Frontinus, *Strategies* 4.7.1; Tacitus, *Annals* 15.16.1, 13.39.1, 15.12.1, 15.3.2.
[24] See the index entry in Y. Le Bohec (ed.), *The Encyclopedia of the Roman Army*, 3 vols, Chichester: Wiley Blackwell, 2015.

cheese, oil, water, wine, vinegar, salt, bread and fruit.[25] Cavalry horses and pack animals also needed considerable fodder. Every Roman fort had its own granary or storehouse (*horreum*), and Tacitus reports that those built by Agricola in Britain could hold a year's supply of grain.[26]

Supplies came from a variety of sources. Grain could be raised from local taxation in kind. In the eastern part of the empire, taxes known as liturgies would be imposed on local elites to help supply an army in transit through the region. Vehicles could be contributed by Italian allies, built by craftsmen in the army camps themselves, or captured from the enemy.[27] Clothing came mainly from Sicily, Sardinia and Spain and this helped to diversify the supply of the army and prevented it from becoming overly reliant on one supplier.[28] The transportation of resources was carried out by similarly various means, with ships, trucks, pack animals and slaves all being used as well as the soldiers themselves, the so-called Marian mules.

Supply patterns varied, depending on certain factors.[29] Being in friendly or hostile territory required different approaches to supply, as did being on the march or in camp. Campaigns often advanced along the course of a river line because it made supply from the rear easier.[30] Overland supply was also frequently needed, although this presented an attractive target for the enemy and required protection. Vegetius warns that in securing provisions, 'careful consideration should be given to supplies and costs' to ensure that they will be available.[31] A balance had to be struck between supply and speed, since the vulnerability of a military column increases in direct proportion to the size of the baggage train.[32]

Supply lines focused on operational, tactical and strategic bases. Operational supplies represented those gathered within the area of operation itself and were usually held in warehouses in a port. Once these supplies were transported to the army itself in the field, these were stored in tactical bases for the army to use as required. Strategic bases were used to store significant reserves of supplies, with grain being kept for up to ten years.[33] The focus on maintaining key strategic reserves allowed for speedy reinforcement and the free flow of resources along carefully prepared lines

---

[25] See J. P. Roth, *The Logistics of the Roman Army at War (264 B.C.–A.D. 235)*, Leiden: Brill, 1999, pp. 18–43; and P. Erdkamp, *Hunger and the Sword: Warfare and Food Supply in Roman Republican Wars (264–30 B.C.)*, Amsterdam: J. C. Gieben, 1998.
[26] Tacitus, *Agricola* 22. [27] See, for example, Livy 27.43.10–11, 36.40.11.
[28] Livy 29.36.2–3, 30.3.2, 32.27.2.
[29] See J. Peddie, *The Roman War Machine*, Stroud: Alan Sutton, 1994.
[30] See, for example, Tiberius using the Elbe, *Velleius Paterculus* 2.106.
[31] Vegetius, *Epitome of Military Matters* 3.3 de copiis expensisque sollers debet esse tractatus.
[32] Peddie, *The Roman War Machine*, p. 47. [33] Livy 42.12.8.

of communication, especially in an emergency. The complexity of these supply networks is illustrated in Tacitus' description of Nero's general Domitius Corbulo's campaign in Armenia in 56–8 CE.[34] Supplies were shipped across the Black Sea, passing through the operational base at Trapezus, before being conveyed 125 miles over the anti-Taurus mountains to the Erzerum plateau, from where they were taken by boat along the Araxes river to the army itself stationed near Artaxarta.[35]

Operational supplies were organised by the commander in charge of the army. Indeed, logistical skill was part of being a good general.[36] Military manuals emphasise the need to secure supply lines from attacks, and any movement of the army needed to be planned carefully to avoid it becoming cut off. Vegetius highlights the importance of building camps to have a place to retreat to for protection. An army would seek to establish a degree of self-sufficiency when on campaign in hostile territory, by means such as producing its own weapons within the camp and foraging for food; but forced requisitions – the involuntary seizure or purchase of goods – represented the staple of military logistics. A commander's imperium gave him the power to force citizens to supply the army and thereby reduce the accompanying dangers to foraging in enemy territory.[37] If this descended into uncontrolled pillaging, then the risk was that the soldiers might actually destroy the very provisions they were looking to secure. Attacking enemy logistics represented a key aim. Caesar's account of his campaigns highlights how spies would be used to gain intelligence about enemy supplies, which would then be targeted.[38] Once defeated, an enemy would be stripped of all kinds of resources that would help the occupying Roman army.[39] Some of these would be specified in treaties, which would have the dual effect of simultaneously strengthening Roman forces while weakening the enemy.[40] All these operational measures involved a great deal of ad hoc response to whatever situation the Roman forces found themselves in, but it is clear that these actions were designed to reduce the risk of the army becoming cut off from supplies or, in the event that did happen, from running out of resources altogether.

Overall control of the supply of the army sat with the Senate. The senators' job was to oversee treaties with allies, which might include supply commitments and grants of authority to provincial governors to maintain the supply network in their area. Where the state was unable to provide

---

[34] Tacitus, *Annals* 13.39. [35] Roth, *The Logistics of the Roman Army at War*, p. 168.
[36] E.g., Tacitus, *Agricola* 19. [37] Sallust, *Catiline War* 29.3. [38] Caesar, *Civil War* 3.47.
[39] E.g., Livy 23.32.14–15. [40] E.g., Polybius, *Histories* 15.18.6.

certain supplies, private contractors were used to make good the shortfall.[41] Livy gives two interesting examples, one where these contractors demanded insurance on their cargo and another of a fraud relating to this being discovered, both of which highlight an understanding of the risks involved and the possibilities for fraud they raised.[42] In the first, three groups of contractors who were tendering for contracts to supply the army demanded that the cargoes they shipped should be insured by the state against storm or capture by the enemy. Livy condemns the lack of patriotism of these private contractors but the state acceded to their demands. In the second, two contractors, condemned by Livy for their dishonesty and greed, had obtained a similar state underwriting of their supplies to the army. They then invented stories of shipwrecks to claim the value of the cargoes or placed small and worthless goods on barely seaworthy ships, which were then scuttled out at sea. False declarations were made as to the value of the lost cargoes. It is also noteworthy that the Senate had ignored it when the scam had first been reported, perhaps because it accepted that a certain degree of fraud was inevitable and it did not want to offend the entire contractor class. The Roman people, however, reacted strongly and the tribunes brought a prosecution that, after much disturbance, resulted in a punishment of exile being imposed.

The shift to empire may have seen some replacement of Rome-based contractors to supply the army with a provincial civil administration but this should not be exaggerated.[43] The standing army of the empire, placed mostly along the borders, certainly required a steady flow of supplies, whereas the Republican period saw greater reliance on preparing adequate logistical support in advance of any offensive campaign, but this difference was largely a function of the nature of the kind of military activities being undertaken. Both periods relied on a combination of elaborate logistical infrastructure and ad hoc responses to local situations.

The empire saw a heightened emphasis on the need for speedy communications. The State Post (*cursus publicus*) was set up by the emperor Augustus to enable his messengers to travel swiftly across the empire by means of the road network. Regularly positioned inns would supply rest,

---

[41] E.g., Livy 24.18.10–11, 34.6.13–15, 23.48.4–12, 44.16.3–4.   [42] Livy 23.49.1–3, 25.3.8–4.11.
[43] See P. Sabin et al., *The Cambridge History of Greek and Roman Warfare*, 2 vols, Cambridge: Cambridge University Press, 2007, esp. D. Rathbone, 'Military finance and supply', vol. 2, pp. 158–76, pp. 165–73 on equipment and supplies. Also, P. Erdkamp (ed.), *A Companion to the Roman Army*, Oxford: Blackwell, 2007, esp. P. Kehne, 'War- and Peacetime logistics: supplying imperial armies in East and West', pp. 323–38. He notes that there was no uniform or universal system of military supply, p. 326.

repairs and fresh horses, which enabled a messenger to travel about fifty miles per day. The expense of providing such services fell upon the locality in which the inn sat, with the exception of Italy where it was paid for by the treasury. Much of the traffic carried in this way related to administrative matters of government, but the road network also provided a means of fast information exchange in times of war that could prove vital in preempting or responding to external threats.

It is clear that the Romans put considerable effort into developing a complex supply network that provided the army with significant resources. The sources of these supplies were, however, diverse, although that diversity meant that a high degree of adaptability was built into the system. The system required an in-depth understanding of the level of resources required as well as the ability to plan and administer their supply. It also needed an awareness of the risks posed by hostile military action. The local commander could always draw on a range of responses as he deemed necessary, which allowed for great flexibility and reduced the army's reliance on any single source of supplies.

Law

Legal Uncertainty

Law stands as one of Roman culture's great achievements.[44] Developed over a period of a thousand years, it grew into a highly sophisticated system. One of its functions was to provide a rational method to deal with various uncertainties. In this section I focus on certain legal areas to highlight the ways in which the law was used to impose some level of rational control on what we would call risk.

To begin with, it is worth emphasising just how sophisticated a system Roman law became. Starting with the early Republican laws of the Twelve Tables (*Lex duodecim tabularum*), then the later Republican public laws

---

[44] Useful introductions to Roman law can be found in D. Johnston, *Roman Law in Context*, Cambridge: Cambridge University Press, 2nd edition, 2022, or in greater detail in D. Johnston (ed.), *The Cambridge Companion to Roman Law*, Cambridge: Cambridge University Press, 2015; and P. J. du Plessis, C. Ando and K. Tuori (eds), *The Oxford Handbook of Roman Law and Society*, Oxford: Oxford University Press, 2016. Other good introductions are A. Watson, *The Spirit of Roman Law*, Athens, GA: University of Georgia Press, 1995, and A. M. Riggsby, *Roman Law and the Legal World of the Romans*, Cambridge: Cambridge University Press, 2010. A detailed textbook on Roman law itself from its 'Golden Age' can be found in F. Schulz, *Classical Roman Law*, Oxford: Clarendon, 1951. For an accessible account, see J. Toner, *Infamy: The Crimes of Ancient Rome*, London: Profile, 2019.

(*Leges publicae*), Praetor's edicts and decrees of the Senate (*Senatus consulta*), the law flourished in the early imperial period. This 'golden age' of Roman law is found in the writings of three principal jurists: Gaius, whose *Institutes* date from the second century CE; Ulpian, who lived from 170 to 223/4 CE and wrote the *Regulae*; and Paulus, whose *Sententiae* probably date from c. 200 CE. The various imperial legal pronouncements were later collected in various codes such as the *Theodosian Code*, which contains imperial enactments from 312–438 CE. Above all, the *Corpus Juris Civilis* (body of civil law) was collected by Tribonian on the orders of the emperor Justinian and issued between 529 and 534 CE; it consists of four parts: the *Digest*, *Institutes*, *Code* and *New Constitutions*. The first three served as revisions of existing law, while the final part dealt with Justinian's own enactments. The *Digest* consists of fifty large volumes and contains juristic discussions of previous cases and judgements that were given regarding them, as well as sundry opinions on points of law.

Roman law dealt primarily with private concerns: private property, business contracts and family inheritance. This is called the civil law – the law relating to citizens. Criminal law, by contrast, concerned those offences that were seen as a wrong against all of society and so demanded a public legal action. Only one of the books of the *Digest* deals with criminal law. The aim of civil law was to redress the negative effect of any wrongdoing. So, in the case of a contract, if someone failed to pay the agreed price then the civil law would simply ensure that the correct fee was paid, possibly with some element of compensation for any other negative effects of the non-payment. Once the law started to consider possible future outcomes and who would bear the liability for these, it had to deal with ideas of probability and the potential for future danger, both of which relate closely to the modern notion of risk.

Law dealt with uncertainty through words not numbers.[45] At the heart of the process sat the notion of judgement. The judge had to decide whose evidence to believe and in making that judgement provided a precedent for future decisions about what was likely to be the correct way to settle the dispute. To be convicted of a criminal offence brought with it a high degree of social stigma, which meant that the standard of proof was set high. Most Anglo-Saxon countries follow the formulation of a prosecution

---

[45] On pre-modern ways of dealing with uncertainty, see J. Franklin, *The Science of Conjecture: Evidence and Probability before Pascal*, Baltimore, MD: Johns Hopkins University Press, 2001, and R. Brown, 'History versus Hacking on probability', *History of European Ideas*, 8 (1987), 655–73.

case having to be proved beyond reasonable doubt, aiming to ensure, in other words, that it is highly improbable to be wrong. Roman law set a lower bar but still favoured generosity towards the accused: 'In doubtful matters, the more benevolent opinion is to be preferred', and 'it is better to permit the crimes of a guilty person to go unpunished than to condemn one who is innocent'.[46] The burden of proof lay with the accuser and there were explicit rules on what counted as acceptable evidence. What constituted a good witness, for example, could be affected by personal characteristics such as social status, wealth or reputation. By contrast, other classes of witness were not to be believed, such as slaves.[47]

Significant emphasis was placed on the judge's ability to use his intuition to cut through the uncertainty and discern the truth. The *Digest* is clear that a judicial inquiry should not only look at one type of evidence; rather, the judge had to form an opinion 'as to what you believe to have been proved, or what you may think has not been satisfactorily established, through the exercise of your own judgement'.[48] Great emphasis was placed on producing witnesses, as these were often felt to be a better guide to the truth than other forms of evidence. A rescript from the emperor Hadrian (r. 117–38), from the same section of the *Digest*, states that he rejected a case because no witnesses had been brought before him and he was 'accustomed to examine witnesses'. He was used to assessing the reliability of witnesses and placed great confidence in his ability to do so accurately.

Roman law understood that it was dealing with doubt and uncertainty with regard to evidence but it did not contain any theoretical discussion of probability. It accepted that the judge must sometimes decide which version of events is more likely to be true or nearest to the truth. If all witnesses were of equal integrity and reputation, then such a judgement need not rest on the quantity of witnesses on each side but on their quality. The judge should assess the sincerity of the witnesses as well as which evidence appears to be 'more illuminated with the light of truth'.[49] It became a question of confidence rather than certainty. We have an example of the practical difficulties this raised from the second-century writer Aulus Gellius, who gives an account of his own experience as a judge. He describes how a claimant appeared before him demanding money from another. He had no documentary evidence or witnesses of the debt but, it was evident to Gellius, was a 'thoroughly good man, whose

---

[46] *Digest* 50.17.56 semper in dubiis benigniora praeferenda sunt; 48.19.5 pr.
[47] *Digest* 22.5.3, 48.18.1.16, 22.5.21.   [48] *Digest* 22.5.3.1.
[49] *Digest* 22.5.21.3; cf. 22.5.1.2, 22.3.13.

integrity was proven and well-known, and who led a blameless life'. By contrast, his opponent was shown to be a liar and a cheat. But he was backed up by lawyers, a bunch of 'noisy advocates' who demanded that the usual documentary evidence be produced. Unsure of what to do, Gellius asked some friends in the legal profession for advice. They said the advocates were correct and that the claim should be dismissed. But, Gellius says, 'when I contemplated the men, one full of honesty, the other thoroughly shameful and degraded ... I could not by any means be argued into an acquittal'. Instead, he ordered the case to be postponed and turned to a philosopher for advice. The philosopher agreed that he should find in favour of the honest man. But Gellius was worried that, as a young man, he would acquire a bad reputation if he passed judgement on the grounds of character rather than from evidence. So, still unwilling to find in favour of a bad man, a man who lived 'a most shameful and degraded life', he swore that the case was unclear to him and so passed the matter on to another judge.[50]

This is an interesting case because it can be read in contrasting ways. It could be interpreted to show that judges were more concerned with litigants' moral character than with the facts of the case. This would inevitably have resulted in their favouring those of higher status or those with whom they had some personal connection. Gellius tries to resist this urge and stick to the facts, but does he record the case to show how much better he was than the average judge? Or could it be read as saying the very opposite? Everyone involved in the case, from claimants to lawyers to the judge, knew that evidence was required for any decision. No doubt a judge's assessments of character might nudge the decision one way or the other (as it still does today), but Roman law, in this view, was fundamentally concerned with the facts. It is impossible to know which reading is correct and in many ways the story relies on the tension that existed within the legal system between fact and judicial judgement. But either way, we have a strong sense that both the documentary and character evidence should be weighed up by the judge before making his assessment about which to believe.

The wide discretionary powers of the judge meant that he became a source of risk himself, in that his decision was hard to predict. One interesting document that sheds light on how governors were perceived is the *Interpretation of Dreams* by Artemidorus. The interpretations work by establishing mental equivalences between people and things. So to

---

[50] *Attic Nights* 14.2.4–11, after Loeb translation.

dream of a pure, translucent river flowing gently was good for slaves and defendants in a law case because 'rivers are like masters and judges since they do whatever they like, on a whim, and do not provide any explanation'. Flooded rivers signify cruel judges because of their violence, threats and the great noise they make.[51]

Roman law displays a clear understanding of the idea of something being more probable than another. This often required active interpretation by the judge of what had been previously intended. In one case concerning a disputed will, the judge decides what he thinks the testator had probably intended, using the term *'vero similius'* or 'closer to the truth'.[52] In another case, where a woman and her baby died in a shipwreck, and the granting of her estate depended on which of them had died first, the judge decided it was more likely that the baby predeceased its mother on account of its age, again using the term *'verisimile'* (*quia verisimile videbatur ante matrem infantem perisse*).[53] Or the judge could make a presumption about what would have happened, based upon what could be assumed to have been the case unless there was evidence to the contrary.[54] Whenever matters were unclear, whatever was more likely or usual should be accepted (*in obscuris inspici solere, quod verisimilius est aut quod plerumque fieri solet*).[55]

Roman law saw probability as a matter of legal argument. It was not something to which a mathematical number could be assigned.[56] Legal argument was based on the skills of rhetoric and sought to persuade the listener towards a particular interpretation. As Franklin notes, this represented a blurring of the probable with the plausible, which confused the logical with the psychological. It was not an understanding of probability that displayed any statistical basis but it was still a carefully and rationally developed system which dealt with the idea of probability in a practical way.

One problem Roman judges always faced was the nature of the evidence available to them, and Roman law understood that there was a risk of their being wrong. We can see this in how they treated evidence of theft. The primary distinction was between 'manifest' and 'non-manifest' theft, which meant whether the thief had been caught in the act or not. This largely depended on how close to the scene of the crime the thief was caught, although exactly where the line could be drawn was not specified.

---

[51] Artemidorus, *The Interpretation of Dreams* 2.27. [52] *Digest* 30.96; cf. 35.1.36.1.
[53] *Digest* 23.4.26. [54] *Digest* 34.3.28.3, 41.3.44.4. [55] *Digest* 50.17.114.
[56] See Franklin, *The Science of Conjecture*, p. 102.

If a thief was caught with a stolen item just outside the house from which it was taken, it would count as a manifest theft, but a few miles away it would not. The punishment was more severe for manifest theft for the simple reason that once someone was out of sight, then the degree to which they were plainly culpable declined and the Romans did not want to punish fully someone who might have been innocent. This recognition of the significant possibility that evidence could be unreliable was also reflected in the strange rite that was held for the discovery of stolen goods, known as the 'plate and loincloth search'. The victim had to walk semi-naked through the suspect's premises while holding a plate, the point of which was to prevent the victim from touching any evidence, or indeed planting it.

Future Liabilities

Roman law's focus on civil law reflected society's desire to settle disputes and competing claims among the propertied class. Since many of these revolved around what might happen in the future and which party would be liable for such eventualities, we can use legal texts as a way of understanding how the Romans tried to deal with such uncertainty in a systematic way.

The importance of the legal process in assigning liability for possible future events was not of interest only to the academic lawyers cited in the *Digest*. Vitruvius emphasises that architects required some legal knowledge so that their buildings might not become subject to legal suits relating to matters such as common walls.[57] A type of contract widely used in construction work, *locatio conductio*, specified that the parties agreed to carry out certain tasks and were liable if they did not fulfil their obligations correctly or to a satisfactory standard. In the case of building contracts, the conductor had to complete the works but had also to ensure that they were satisfactorily and carefully carried out. This liability was, however, limited to future normal circumstances and so would not extend to extreme events such as earthquakes.[58] In this situation the liability lay with the owner of the property since suffering from a natural disaster was an inherent risk in property ownership and no builder could reasonably be held to account if

---

[57] See Ronin, 'The perception of natural risks', Vitruvius, *On Architecture* 1.1.10. In this case, the liability lies with the owner, the pater familias, not with the architect. See n.36 for cases where a conductor is released from his responsibility.

[58] *Digest* 19.2.59.

his construction fell down as a result. The text uses the Latin term *periculum* (danger) to describe this risk: the danger belongs to the owner. We can speculate that no more detailed term was required because there was no attempt to quantify the probability of such a disastrous event happening, only to decide who bore the liability if it did. 'Danger' therefore became the standard legal term employed in contracts to indicate the risk of a loss.[59]

An extreme event such as an earthquake made it easy to absolve the builder from any liability. Other situations were more problematic. In a discussion of a legal action concerning damage not yet done but that threatened one's property, the legal commentators note that earthquakes or floods cannot be blamed on the builder, but that if roof tiles were dislodged by the wind from a house and caused injury, the builder would be liable if this occurred because of a defect in the building but not if it occurred because of the violence of the wind.[60] The ultimate cause of the event was something that would have to be decided by the judge based on the balance of probabilities.

Jurists also recognised that the likelihood of something happening could be increased by human actions. Ronin discusses the example of a manmade work (*opus manu factum*), in this case involving the threat posed by a human action, such as a dam or drain, which alters the course or strength of the flow of water and thereby exacerbates the negative impact of naturally occurring rainwater.[61] We can imagine that these were common issues in a largely agricultural society, where land exploitation resulted in an increase in various potentially dangerous outcomes. The increasing probability of such negative events in line with human activity is clearly recognised by the legal opinions and the law can be seen as a way for Roman society to manage the risks that competing interests would generate in their desire to increase the yield from their land. This management aspect is reinforced by the fact that the law relates to the potential for future damage, rather than rectifying something that has already happened. This suggests that all parties were well aware that their own and others' actions relating to water-management practices had the potential to increase the likelihood that some harm would result and so took steps to limit that potential in advance. If the case were brought successfully, then the defendant would have to carry out remedial works to restore the water

---

[59] See G. MacCormack, 'Periculum', *Zeitschrift der Savigny-Stiftung für Rechtsgeschichte:Romanistische Abteilung*, 96 (1979), 129–72.
[60] *Digest* 39.2.24.   [61] *Digest* 39.3.1.

flow to its previous level and thereby remove the risk of a negative event taking place. By contrast, the view that no individual could be held liable for natural water flow showed that there was an acceptance that some level of risk was normal and unavoidable. As another opinion states, when bad things happen naturally, 'each party must endure the consequences with equanimity whether his individual circumstances are thereby improved or worsened'.[62]

The Roman legal understanding of risk referred to that which lay beyond the limits of contractual liability.[63] When the financial loss arising from a breach of contract could not be attributed to either party, but occurred owing to an unforeseen and uncontrollable event (usually described as *vis maior* or *casus fortuitus*), the loss could not be legally attributed to either side. In other words, liability resulted from one party's fault, whereas risk reflected that which was nobody's fault. On this understanding, risk became an almost detachable entity, and in purchase contracts a point was specified at which risk passed from the seller to buyer, normally the point at which the goods were delivered.[64] The jurist Paul distinguishes between different kinds of risk (*vitium*) in the context of the construction of a channel, and in doing so shows that 'risk' may shift from one party to another.[65] This was not an understanding of risk defined in abstract terms, since it was closely linked to fact-based scenarios and also to standard commercial practice.[66] Similarly, employment contracts relating to dangerous work, such as in mining, do not refer to a generic term to indicate the risk involved in carrying out these difficult tasks but specify what the principal danger is in each situation, such as flooding or fire.

Legal texts use a variety of terms to cover what we would call risk – *periculum*, *vis maior*, *casus fortuitus*, *vitium* – and their usage developed over time.[67] It would be an exaggeration to say that the development of sophisticated legal terminology meant that the Romans had a sophisticated

---

[62] *Digest* 39.3.2.6 aequo animo unumquemque ferre debere, siue melior siue deterior eius condicio facta sit.
[63] P. J. Du Plessis, *Letting and Hiring in Roman Legal Thought 27BCE–284CE*, Leiden: Brill, 2012, pp. 24–5. See also É. Jakab, 'Risikomanagement bei den Naukleroi', in N. Benke and F.-S. Meissel (eds), *Antike – Recht – Geschichte*, Frankfurt: P. Lang, 2009, pp. 73–88; and *Risikomanagement beim Weinkauf: Periculum und Praxis im Imperium Romanum*, Munich: C. H. Beck, 2009; G. MacCormack, 'Dolus, culpa, custodia and diligentia – criteria of liability or content of obligation', *Index*, 22 (1996), 189–209.
[64] *Digest* 17.1.39.   [65] *Digest* 19.2.62.
[66] See Jakab, *Risikomanagement beim Weinkauf*, pp. 43–4; 'should inundation impact the work he shall calculate a proportional reduction of the wages'.
[67] Du Plessis, *Letting and Hiring*, pp. 38–9; see also G. MacCormack, 'Further on Periculum', *BIDR*, 1979 (1982), 11–40 on various legal meanings of the term *periculum* in Roman law.

abstract understanding of the various elements of risk. *Periculum*, for example, did not refer only to a financial loss that had occurred without fault but also to the possibility of a loss. Often there is a conceptual link between *periculum* and *vitium*. *Vis maior* generally represented a force that was superior to humans and therefore could not be taken into account in determining liability, such 'acts of God' being defined in one opinion as 'Superior force, which the Greeks call "Divine Power"'. The opinion also shows, however, that the meaning of the term was open to interpretation, stating that a tenant farmer should not suffer a loss where the crops are damaged 'to an unusual degree', but if the damage was only moderate he should put up with it 'with untroubled mind'.[68] Ultimately, where the risk lay was up to the judge to decide. But throughout, jurists accepted that unforeseeable events should not operate to the detriment of only one party to a contract, which suggests that they understood that the idea of future danger should be treated separately from other aspects of the contract. By the time the jurist Ulpian was writing in the early third century CE, it had become standard practice in contracts for letting and hiring, for example, to attribute any unforeseen loss to the owner of the property.[69]

We can see this also in contracts for consensual sale and the idea of *periculum emptoris*.[70] Numerous situations arose in commerce, particularly as Roman trade across the Mediterranean increased, where a simple cash transaction was not possible. For reasons of transportation, for example, the moment of delivery of goods would postdate the agreement between buyer and seller to transact the business, or problems of payment might arise if the buyer was unable to access immediate sources of credit. In such cases, the two parties would agree to delay the transaction but accepted that a legal obligation existed between them, which would be specified in the contract with regard to such matters as the price, quantity and quality of goods, as well as the size of any down payment, and was actionable if either party broke their side of the bargain. Instead of treating the act of sale as a single event, Roman law specified that it comprised two separate parts. The first was the agreement to transact. The second was the conveyance of the contracted goods to the new owner. The down payment would be non-refundable in the event of the buyer pulling out of the deal and can be seen as covering some or all of the seller's costs should that happen. Since going to court was, as ever, an onerous business, the deposit

---

[68] *Digest* 19.2.25.6.   [69] *Digest* 4.9.3.1.
[70] See R. Yaron, 'Remarks on consensual sale (with special attention to periculum emptoris)', *Roman Legal Tradition*, 59 (2004), 59–76.

also functioned as a deterrent against such breaking of the contract and, depending on its size, as a punitive cost in addition. Generally, the larger the deal the greater the deposit demanded by the seller. We can see that Roman law recognised that both parties were risking something – the buyer that the seller would not deliver, the seller that the buyer would not pay – and so provided a legal mechanism that effectively provided insurance against that risk.

The delay in the transaction between the initial agreement and the point of delivery also created an additional risk: that the goods would be damaged or destroyed in transit, never a remote risk given the demands of ancient sea-travel. The law had to decide who would bear the loss in such an eventuality. It is worth noting that such situations would most often involve *vis maior*, since storms at sea were obviously beyond the control of either party. The law favoured the seller since the benefits of ownership had already passed from the seller to the buyer at the point of agreement and drawing up of the contract. If the value of the goods rose during the period between contract and delivery, all the financial upside accrued to the buyer even though the seller had to deal with the problems of storage and transport. It was therefore decided to counterbalance the benefits and that any loss should be borne by the buyer, and the risk that this might happen was termed the *periculum emptoris*. This meant that, if all the goods were lost, the buyer would still have to pay the full agreed price, even though actual ownership was delayed until the moment the goods were handed over. It was possible for both parties to agree to exclude *periculum emptoris* from the contract but this would have to be done explicitly. Sales of wine, for example, were often excluded because it frequently went off during storage or transport.[71]

Certain contracts relating to future purchases could throw up interesting legal dilemmas. A simple form of futures contract existed where it was possible to purchase goods in advance of their being produced, such as buying a fisherman's catch ahead of his putting out to sea. The legal question then arose as to what liability would exist should the fisherman refuse to go to sea. As the legal opinion states, 'the uncertainty of the result must be taken into account in assessing the damages'. Since the size of the catch could not be known in advance, any recompense would have to take into account this uncertainty. Or, if the fisherman refused to hand over his

---

[71] R. Yaron, 'Sale of wine', in D. Daube (ed.), *Studies in the Roman Law of Sale*, Oxford: Clarendon, 1959, pp. 71–7.

catch, the judge would have to estimate how big his catch had been.[72] All of these judgements depended upon rational estimations about what was likely to happen or have happened, primarily based upon past experience.

Future Ownership

Death is, of course, certain but the Romans made considerable efforts to limit the effects of the uncertainty that exists over its timing and consequences and to ensure the orderly handover of a deceased individual's assets. This concern was most notable among Rome's wealthy, to such an extent that Cato the Elder listed the single day he had once been intestate as one of his main regrets in life.[73] An exaggeration, no doubt, but not much of one given the huge quantity of testamentary legal discussion found in no fewer than nine of the fifty books of the *Digest*. The primary reason for this high level of concern with making a will was the need to have an heir who would continue the family line and, in doing so, maintain the communal identity of which the testator was a part. The high level of mortality in the Roman world and the unpredictability of when an individual might die can only have exacerbated these anxieties. It must have been common for children to have predeceased their fathers, while many others will have had no offspring. But wills were never only about passing wealth to the first born. Bequests also provided the opportunity to benefit friends and relatives, as well to reward loyal slaves and freedmen, in a way that maintained the family's reputation by dispersing property among a wider group consisting of extended kin and peers.

The problem with making a will, however, was that it had certain legal restrictions which made it less useful as a vehicle to achieve this wealth dispersion. A will had to have an heir or heirs who were entitled to receive the entire estate (less any legacies). The will had to be drawn up using certain vocabulary expressing a direct command and it had to be written in Latin. It also had to be witnessed by adult male Roman citizens. It could also grant a usufruct only to a specific individual, rather than to as yet unborn descendants. In addition, the *lex Falcidia*, of 41 BCE, regulated the contents of a will, decreeing that the heir must receive at least one-quarter of the estate, while other legacies could not total more than three-quarters. Augustan laws also limited the number of slaves that an individual could free in their will to a certain percentage depending on the total number of slaves owned. Above all, various groups of people were prevented from

---

[72] *Digest* 19.11.18, 19.12.   [73] Plutarch, *Cato the Elder* 9.6.

benefiting from legacies made in a will. This included *incertae personae*, that is to say descendants as yet unborn, foreigners and Julian Latins. Following Augustus' marriage laws of 18 and 9 BCE, it also included unmarried adults, while childless married couples could receive only half of what they had been left.

Many wealthy individuals therefore sought an alternative means of passing on wealth after their demise that allowed them a greater degree of control of where their assets went. The *fideicommissum* served to achieve these aims, which allowed assets to be entrusted to the good faith of the recipient, for the benefit of another individual. This is clearly similar to a modern-day trust. It allowed an individual to give assets to a much broader range of individuals than a will and, because of this flexibility that it allowed, became a widely used vehicle for controlling the future ownership of family wealth.[74] In the case of Augustus' marriage laws, for example, a father could leave assets to his unmarried daughter via a trusted friend. Trusts also allowed assets to be handed down through the generations by requiring the recipient to pass assets on to as yet unborn descendants. It also allowed masters to pass on the act of manumitting slaves to another, thereby avoiding the legal restrictions concerning the number of slaves being freed. The *fideicommissum* was also a far more informal arrangement, requiring only words requesting the trusted individual to carry out the task.[75] It did not even need to be written down, although in practice these requests were often listed in a will or codicil.

It might seem that the principal risk was that the entrusted individual would fail to carry out what was requested of him. Since the trust was not part of established law, there was no legal obligation on the part of the entrusted individual to carry out the deceased's wishes. In practice, however, this was unlikely, partly because of the reputational risk involved in not doing so. But *fideicommissa* were also enforceable, since they represented fiduciary agreements premised on bona fides. Failure to carry out the deceased's wishes could result in *infamia*, which excluded an individual from making commercial actions. This legally binding nature was formally admitted by the emperor Augustus.[76]

What the *fideicommissum* allowed, above all, was deadhand control: the ability of the deceased to continue to control where wealth went. The bequest, for example, could direct the recipient to transfer the asset at death to the next generation. No matter how feckless an heir might be, it

---

[74] See D. Johnston, *The Roman Law of Trusts*, Oxford: Clarendon, 1988. [75] *Institutes* 2.23.2.
[76] *Institutes* 2.23.1.

was therefore possible to prevent them from disposing of the asset while living. One text goes even further, requesting that 'I wish my house not to be sold by my heirs nor to be pledged by them but to remain intact with them and their sons and descendants for all time'.[77] This is, however, the only example of a perpetual bequest in the *Digest*, probably because Roman law did not permit settlements in perpetuity and restricted the testator to handing down his assets for one generation. The ability to maintain deadhand control was therefore limited to the immediate beneficiaries and any further children born later. This may reflect that the other main purpose of the trust was not simply to pass on an entire family patrimony but to ensure that everyone who the deceased felt deserved a bequest, whatever their legal status, should benefit, in order to maintain the family's reputation.

In concluding this section on law, we can say that legal discourse represented an intellectual means of understanding, ordering and ascribing risk. Rather than probabilistic calculation, it relied on verbal argument and reasoning, but much of the legal discussion does not separate risk out as an abstract concept, preferring instead to reify it as part of practical assessments of liability and likelihood. There is, for that reason, no clear definition of risk provided or specific understanding that is as exact or detailed as modern calculative approaches. But the law did offer some detailed cases which moved significantly along the spectrum of understanding towards those more modern ideas.

Financial Management

Various kinds of what we might term financial risk control can also be discerned in various Roman activities. I focus on three areas that are all related to interest rates: interest rates themselves, maritime loans and annuities. This is an area where Roman calculations most closely approximate to modern numerical notions relating to risk. The aim is to show that the assumptions employed in their investment decisions suggest a good level of understanding of the underlying risks.

Roman investors had a variety of investment opportunities, most notably agricultural land, rental property, lending money for interest and trade. The returns they achieved on these investments will have differed significantly at various periods but the Romans had limited accounting skills to calculate these accurately. Columella, for example, discusses the returns

---

[77] *Digest* 31.88.15.

available on vines without taking into account any depreciation or production costs, and his estimate of profits is therefore overstated.[78] However, if we look at his calculation we can see two areas where there is an understanding of certain aspects of the different risks involved in this investment:

1. Investment risk. The investment should 'enrich the owner'. Columella is aware that the investment should give a positive yield and that there is a risk that it will not. If the investor does not believe it will be profitable, he should not invest.
2. Relative risk. Columella notes that many prefer to own pastures or woodland, because they believe the yield will be greater. His calculation understands that the return should exceed the cost of capital, since otherwise it would be better simply to lend the money at the prevailing annual rate of 6 per cent.
3. Income risk. Columella understands that yields from investments can rise and fall. He argues that 'the return from vineyards is a very rich one' and refers to Varro as having the same view that each *iugerum* of land (c. 0.25 of a hectare) will yield 600 *urnae* of wine (c. 1,700 UK gallons). But he argues that viticulture is being overlooked by investors because yields have often been below that level on account of poor farming techniques. By contrast, he stresses that better cultivation will result in substantially higher yields.

What is most notably lacking is any awareness of inflation risk. This partly resulted from a limited understanding of the concept of inflation but may also have reflected the short-term nature of most loans. It could be argued that the understanding of investment risk noted earlier included the idea that an investment should generate a real return, over and above inflation, but this is neither articulated as such nor, indeed, expressed in any oblique way.

Interest Rates

Columella does show that lending money for interest was common practice. Even though much of this lending was influenced by social factors and carried out interest-free as an act of friendship between equals, there is

---

[78] Columella 3.3. See R. H. Macve, 'Some glosses on "Greek and Roman accounting"', *History of Political Thought*, 6 (1985), 233–64.

also widespread evidence for loans made at commercial interest rates. Various types of commercial lending took place: both unsecured and secured, but also loans in kind, such as loans of land in return for a share of the harvest. The high interannual variation in crop yield and the frequent imposition of sudden taxes 'all reinforced a pattern of borrowing and dependence'.[79] The majority of loans involved small quantities and were short term, for less than year, serving to smooth out these fluctuations in income among those of modest means. The main reason for this thriving debt market was obviously that it was profitable. Loans backed by prime Italian land could be raised at 6 per cent, as Columella notes, whereas unsecured, short-term loans could cost as much as 50 per cent.[80] Twelve per cent is by far the most commonly found rate, possibly because it was the simplest to calculate at 1 per cent per month, and was indeed the legal maximum.[81] Looking at these interest rates can also reveal that Roman borrowers and lenders understood a variety of risks relating to the practice.

1. Market risk. The frequency of loans meant that, rather than loans existing only as private agreements between individuals, there was an understanding that there was a market in interest rates that was easily accessible. This made it possible to distinguish between the market rate of interest and the rate on a specific loan. These rates fluctuated according to market conditions, which we would term 'market risk'. The *Digest* displays this understanding when it notes that 'in some places money can be raised easily and at low interest, while in others only with more difficulty and at a high rate of interest'.[82] Similarly, Cicero records an occasion when monthly interest rates moved from 1/3 to 2/3 per cent (i.e., from 4 per cent to 8 per cent per annum).[83] This does not mean that the market was liquid or unaffected by rates being charged at habitual or social rates. Since most loans were not negotiable, or at least they were not bought and sold in practice, there was no understanding that the price of existing loans would move in line with the prevailing market interest rate. But it is clear that, from the perspective of both borrower and lender, the market as a

---

[79] K. Hopkins, *Conquerors and Slaves*, Cambridge: Cambridge University Press, 1978, p. 22.
[80] Cicero, *Letters to Atticus* 5.21.12; *P. Tebt.* 110.
[81] On ancient interest rates, see J. Andreau, *Banking and Business in the Roman World*, Cambridge: Cambridge University Press, 1999, pp. 90–9 and G. Billeter, *Geschichte des Zinsfusses im griechisch-römischen Altertum bis auf Justinian*, Leipzig: Teubner, 1898. An accessible overview can be found in S. Homer and R. Sylla, *A History of Interest Rates*, 3rd edition, New Brunswick: Rutgers University Press, 1991.
[82] *Digest* 13.4.3.   [83] Cicero, *Letters to Atticus* 4.15.7.

whole could move and there were resultant opportunities when credit was cheap or vice versa.

2. Default risk. The *Digest* understood that commercial interest rates compensated the investor for the risk that the borrower would not pay back either the interest or the capital sum. As it says about maritime loans, 'the price is for the peril' (*periculi pretium est*).[84] The level of anxiety this could create in the lender is noted by the fourth-century Christian writer Gregory of Nyssa, in his treatise against usury. He describes how a lender makes sure he is fully appraised of his debtor's position: 'The moneylender is inquisitive with regard to the activities of the person in his debt as well as to his personal travels, activities, movements, and livelihood', and if he 'hears a bad report about anyone who has fallen among thieves or whose good fortune has changed to destitution, the moneylender sits with folded hands, groans continuously, and weeps much.'[85]

There is therefore an awareness that certain other conditions will reduce the level of risk that the lender is undertaking. The first of these is the length of time for which the money is being lent. One law discusses a loan where it was agreed that the borrower would pay a higher rate if he was late with his repayments.[86] This can be seen in part as simply a punitive rate, but it would also reflect the higher risk of default that the lender is incurring when payments are missed. What it does not reflect is any understanding of what we now call a term structure of interest rates, where market rates are freely available for different maturities of loan. There was a wide understanding that default risk could also be reduced by demanding security for the loan. Most often this would take the form of land. The quality of the land would affect the level of the interest rate, with high-quality Italian land attracting a favourable rate of 6 per cent, as in the Columella example.

In the event of default, creditors held considerable legal powers and could sell all the debtor's possessions. A fourth-century papyrus from Egypt describes the case of an indebted wine dealer who could not repay his loans and 'was compelled by his creditors to sell all his possessions

---

[84] *Digest* 22.2.4–5.
[85] Gregory of Nyssa, *Against Usury*, in *Gregorii Nysseri Opera* 9.195–207, with discussion and translation in C. McCambley, 'Against those who practice usury by Gregory of Nyssa', *Greek Orthodox Theological Review*, 36 (1991), 287–302, with minor alterations.
[86] *Digest* 22.1.12.

down to the very garments that cloaked his shame; and even when these were sold, barely half the money could he scrape together for his creditors who ... carried off all his children although they were mere infants.'[87] Another example from Egypt describes how an illiterate weaver inherited her father's debt of 18,000 drachma. Unable to pay the interest on the loan, she was forced to work for her creditor on a full-time basis. Such powers themselves reflect an understanding that lending money involved the taking on of a considerable risk of default.

3. Legal risk. What these legal documents also highlight, however, was that there was legal risk in the business of making loans. The law put limits on interest rates, primarily because of the potential for unrest that excessively high rates could cause. Calls for debt cancellation, *tabulae novae*, featured prominently in popular political demands in the late republic, in provincial uprisings such as the first Jewish revolt and in the regular tax remissions that emperors were forced to grant.[88] The official maximum may have been 1 per cent a month, but there were ways around this, either by simply ignoring it or handing over a smaller sum of money than stipulated in the contract. Defaulting debtors did, however, have the right to appeal to the authorities if they felt they had been cheated by their lenders. One petition from 147 CE (*P. Mich.* 225) criticised the moneylender as being 'reckless in his conduct and violent', and 'committing every impious and forbidden act' by demanding interest at 48 per cent per annum and then trying to recoup his investment by force. The petitioner asks that the legal maximum be enforced. We do not know how this particular case unfolded, and we might assume that the indebted poor were unlikely to be successful in many of their petitions for help from the authorities, but there was evidently a risk for the lender that the law could intervene in their contract and cancel or reduce the payments.

4. Risk premium. This represents the amount of extra interest that is needed to entice investors to take on the added risk of lending money. We can get some idea of how often defaults occurred by looking at the default rate implied by market interest rates.[89] The market rate represents the risk-free rate (in the modern world this would be the interest rate on loans to a central bank) plus a risk premium to compensate the lender for

---

[87] *P. Lond.* 1915, after Loeb translation.
[88] Josephus, *Jewish War* 2.425–7; on tax remissions, see R. Duncan-Jones, *Money and Government in the Roman Empire*, Cambridge: Cambridge University Press, 1994, pp. 59–61.
[89] See Toner, *Popular Culture in Ancient Rome*, pp. 24–6.

the defaults that will be incurred in lending. The calculation for the implied default rate is as follows:

Price = Risk-free Rate × [Cash Flow × Survival Rate + Recovery Rate × Default Rate]

As a fair approximation, we can take the 6 per cent rate for loans backed by premium Italian real estate as the equivalent of the risk-free rate, discounted by one year. We then need to make an assumption about the recovery rate, which is the amount of money the creditor manages to salvage from his debtor's assets in the event of default. The first of the earlier examples from Egypt suggests a recovery rate of about 50 per cent. The default rate represents the percentage that will equalise the risk-free rate with the market rate. So for the standard legal maximum of 12 per cent the calculation is:

Year	Cash Flow	Survival Rate	Default Rate
1	112	90	10

Where: Cash Flow = the repayment of Principal + Interest
Assuming: a Recovery rate of 50 per cent, a Risk-free Rate of 6 per cent (discounted to 5.7) and a Price of 100.

The maximum market interest rate suggests that approximately 10 per cent of borrowers could be expected to go bankrupt each year. In reality, however, this calculation fails to take into account the excess profit (the risk premium) that the market rate will incorporate in order to overcompensate for likely defaults. In theory, the risk premium cannot be too high because other lenders would then enter the market to provide more competitive rates. In practice, the Roman debt market was relatively basic and so is unlikely to have functioned so efficiently. It is also likely that returns will have been cyclical, so that lenders would benefit from a high level of risk premium for most periods but would then suffer losses during any economic downturn.

Given that we lack information on default rates in Rome, it is impossible to calculate the size of the risk premium. The high level of standard interest rates suggests that the risk premium was large, particularly relative to the low level charged for loans secured by Italian land. But the high level of security that was often required and the substantial legal powers of creditors may have meant that the default rate was lower than we might otherwise expect. The conclusion then would be that default risk is overstated by the ancient sources and the risk premium understated.

In either case, it is apparent that the Romans did not explicitly calculate either form of risk but that they understood that there was a risk of default and that interest rates should produce a profit that compensated for taking it on.

5. Risk, return and diversification. One interesting example shows that some investors understood the idea of taking on more risk and leverage to exaggerate their financial returns. Plutarch relates that, when Cato the Elder began to 'apply himself more strenuously to money-making', he came to regard agriculture as 'more entertaining than profitable'. He therefore invested his capital in businesses such as ponds and hot springs for use in the fulling trade, which brought him 'large profits' and could not, to use his own phrase, 'be ruined by Jupiter' or what we would term 'Acts of God'. He also made loans on shipping, but he reduced his risk by forming his borrowers into one company (*societas*), which therefore had a number of ships as security. However, he would take only one share in the business. He therefore managed to reduce his risk both by diversification and by reducing the size of his own capital investment, thereby maintaining a high level of return.[90] The fact that Plutarch reports this activity may mean that it was not common, but it does show that some sophisticated investors were in some sense aware of the relationship between risk and return.

6. Systemic risk. We also have a number of reports of occasions where the financial system itself was imperilled by particular crises. Cicero, for example, noted that, when many investors lost large sums of money in Asia, the supply of credit in Rome dried up as a consequence: 'the loss of the one inevitably undermines the other and causes its collapse'.[91] As he also noted, any serious dissent in Asia caused a panic in the Forum. There was therefore an understanding that the empire's financial markets were connected and could be threatened by a crisis in one of them, even though it was far away. The form of this interconnectedness is unclear but probably involved some form of financial intermediary rather than simply direct person-to-person loans.

Roman loans displayed a level of understanding of the different kinds of financial risk involved in lending. Much of this risk was assessed intuitively rather than being calculated numerically and was all rolled up into one single rate without ever being separated out into its constituent parts. But

---

[90] Plutarch, *Cato the Elder* 21.6.   [91] Cicero, *On Pompey's Command* 14–19.

maritime loans seem to have become more sophisticated than most in the range of risks they assessed, and I now examine them in more detail.

Maritime Loans

The Mediterranean Sea sat at the heart of the Roman empire, and using its waters for transport was always considerably cheaper than land-based alternatives for anything other than short journeys. The sea itself, though, could be a highly unpredictable medium for travel because of uncertain weather, poor-quality shipping and piracy. A sailor's life was therefore synonymous with uncertainty, and writers often express financial bankruptcy in terms of being stuck in a storm and suffering shipwreck.[92] Nor was the uncertainty confined to the sailors. Lending money for sea trade was itself a risky business, and Gregory of Nyssa describes how, '[i]f the usurer has loaned to a sailor, he sits on the shore, worrying about the wind's movement ... and awaiting the report of a wreck or some other misfortune. His soul is disquieted whenever he sees the sea angered.' Financing sea trade was always a high-risk, high-return activity and, as we have seen, Petronius has his vulgar parvenu, Trimalchio, engaging in the business to an excessive degree, epitomising the kind of pushy pleb who the elite thought dominated the trade. Snobbery of this kind also meant that aristocrats, such as Cato, employed agents to carry out this business on their behalf.

The business was varied. Most ships seem to have been owned by shippers who transported and traded goods on their own account. Other merchants hired ships for specific trade voyages. The main problem faced by all traders was the capital outlay required to purchase a hull's worth of goods, which would often cost a multiple of the value of the ship, especially if luxury items were being transported. It would not be possible to recoup their money until the ship had sailed and docked and the goods had been sold, a process which could take anything from a few weeks to a year or more. Most traders either lacked the reserves of money to fund such ventures upfront or did not wish to risk what could be a significant part of their wealth on a single craft. The high level of returns available in such trade attracted finance from wealthy individuals such as Cato. The transaction was complicated by the fact that the trader's ability to repay was dependent on the ship successfully completing its voyage with the

---

[92] Alciphron, *Letters* 1.13; Plutarch, *Moral Essays* 831e.

result that a specific type of legal contract was developed to accommodate this risk, known as the maritime loan (*faenus nauticum*).[93]

Maritime loans were originally a Greek practice but were imported into Roman law. The earlier example of Cato the Elder from the second century BCE is, in fact, the first Roman example we possess. The surviving evidence is thin, but there are various examples in legal texts that discuss a range of both actual and fictional cases.[94] Part of a contract survives concerning arrangements relating to a debt-financed voyage from Alexandria to Muziris on the Malabar coast, and it is possible that this represented the standard text for a maritime loan.[95] The size of this loan, almost seven million sesterces (seven times what was needed to become a senator), gives an idea of how sizeable some of these loans had become by the time of the empire. Such evidence as there is suggests that these loans shared some standard features throughout the long period of their use. The loan was made to a trader to finance a single trading event, usually a round trip. The loan paid for the purchase of a cargo, which the trader would sell and then use the proceeds to repay the loan with interest. The deadline for repayment was within one year. Within this standard framework, a range of variations was possible, such as multiple trips or collective financing. The most common was when the trader also owned the ship, in which case the vessel was used as security for the loan in return for a lower rate of interest. It is apparent that various concepts relating to risk are tied up in these contracts, and we can split these out as having the following effects.

1. Risk Transfer. Trade was a dangerous business and the trader would be able to repay the loan only if he arrived safely at port and sold on his goods. Unlike an ordinary loan, therefore, the maritime contract specified that the borrower did not have to pay either the capital or the interest if the ship and its cargo failed to make it safely to the specified destination. The effect

---

[93] G. E. M. de Ste Croix, 'Ancient Greek and Roman maritime loans', in H. C. Edey and B. S. Yamey (eds), *Debits, Credits, Finance and Profits*, London: Sweet and Maxwell, 1974, pp. 41-59; D. W. Rathbone, 'The financing of maritime commerce in the Roman empire (I–II AD)', in E. Lo Cascio (ed.), *Credito e moneta nel mondo romano*, Bari, Italy: Edipuglia, 2003, pp. 197–229; J. Rougé, 'Prêt et société maritimes dans le monde romain', in J. H. D'Arms and E. C. Kopff (eds), *The Seaborne Commerce of Ancient Rome*, Rome: American Academy in Rome, 1980, pp. 291–303; P. Candy and E. Mataix Ferrándiz (eds), *Roman Law and Maritime Commerce*, Edinburgh: Edinburgh University Press, 2022. On the Greek loans, see P. Millett, 'Maritime loans and the structure of credit in fourth-century Athens', in P. Garnsey, K. Hopkins and C. R. Whittaker (eds), *Trade in the Ancient Economy*, London: Chatto & Windus, 1983, pp. 36–52.

[94] See esp. *Digest* 22.2, 45.1.122; *Justinian Code* 4.33; *Novels* 106, 110.

[95] Rathbone plausibly argues that the various errors resulted from a scribe's careless copying of what was a standard document of its type. See now F. De Romanis, *The Indo-Roman Pepper Trade and the Muziris Papyrus*, Oxford: Oxford University Press, 2020.

was to transfer some of the risk of the venture onto the lender. If the ship was lost, then the lender lost his money, or if the cargo was partly lost, then the principal was reduced accordingly. Clearly there was potential for fraud here, and the law specified that the borrower had to carry out his side of the bargain faithfully, such as by following an agreed route. Any acts by the trader that deliberately harmed the vessel, such as running it aground, would also see the loss transfer back to him. In some cases, it appears that the risk of loss would also transfer back to the trader if he failed to complete his journey by the specified date.[96]

2. Compensating for higher risk. Roman law capped interest rates on normal loans at 12 per cent, but maritime loans were treated as a different case and no limit was applied.[97] This was because it was evident that the level of risk that the investor was undertaking was substantially above that assumed by a normal lender. Not only could the ship be lost but the trader could be fraudulent, and it was difficult to enforce the stipulations of the agreement. The rate of interest was expressed in terms of a yield on a lump sum, with an eighth being the usual for shorter trips, but perhaps because it was seen as usual for the sailing season to allow only one round trip, this yield is often referred to in legal texts as an annual rate of interest.[98] It was customary to allow a grace period after the ship had docked to enable the trader to sell his wares. If the goods were sold for significantly less than had been hoped, the maritime loan would earn a much lower return than originally forecast. We can see, therefore, that the interest rate represented, in effect, a combination of the cost of financing and a share of the profits. Its level was agreed between the two parties and depended upon how hazardous the voyage was, its duration and its distance. The venture represented a business partnership between the financier and the trader and so we can interpret their stakes as being like an equity share in the enterprise, whereby each partner received a share of the profits. Roman law seemed implicitly to recognise this by not enforcing the normal legal maximum rate of interest.

The level of returns actually attained is recorded only from a single Classical Greek example, where a figure of 22.5 per cent is recorded (to be increased to 30 per cent if the trip entailed travel outside the safe summer

---

[96] *Digest* 45.1.122.1.
[97] The exclusion from rate caps for maritime loans was abolished in 528 CE, when Justinian imposed a limit of 12 per cent per annum. See *Novels* 106 and 110.
[98] Of Claudius Flavius Zeuxis (IGRR 4.841) it is said that, 'as a merchant he rounded Cape Malea 72 times on voyages to Italy', which suggests he was making at least two trips per summer.

sailing period).⁹⁹ Given that voyages in the Roman world earned 12.5 per cent, it would have taken two shorter round trips to generate this kind of return, or perhaps a single longer trip sourcing luxury goods from Arabia or India. This high level of return implicitly reflected the dangers involved in the enterprise. Using an implied loss rate, we can calculate that 20 per cent equates to a loss rate of 12 per cent of ships per annum.¹⁰⁰ This figure will overstate the realised loss rate because of the inclusion of a risk premium, which represents the reward for taking on the extra risk involved in maritime lending. If we assume a healthy profit margin of 50–75 per cent, this means that 3–6 per cent of ships were wrecked, which in itself underscores what a risky venture this was for all concerned.

3. Risk reduction. Although maritime loans were clearly high risk, the practices around them also served to reduce the risk of those involved. The lender generally required security for the loan, such as the ship, its equipment and the cargo, although this would all be lost if the ship was lost at sea. The loan was therefore more likely to be backed by some or all the trader's other assets, such as other ships he owned, other goods he possessed or land. In Greek examples, the security seems to have represented a sum of at least twice the value of the loan and it may be that Roman practice was similar. Whatever the collateral, the borrower had to repay only the principal sum of the loan so long as the ship arrived safely at its final destination. The collateral merely reduced the lender's risk that the trader would be fraudulent or refuse to pay, or that the goods would sell for less than their cost.

Risk could also be reduced by means of a collective association (*societas*) as in the earlier example of Cato. By forming a consortium, merchants shared the risk of both profits and losses between themselves. It enabled the individual merchant to pledge as security against the loss of his own ship the cargoes of all of the consortium's ships. Even though the collective cargoes would be pledged to multiple investors, the likelihood of a significant proportion of the consortium's ships being sunk at the same time was small. This added level of security would also most likely have attracted potential investors and so made it easier to raise finance. Investors could also form their own consortium by pooling their funds and distributing the profits in accordance with their share.¹⁰¹

---

⁹⁹ Demosthenes, *Speeches* 35; cf. 32, 34, 56.
¹⁰⁰ See Toner, *Popular Culture in Ancient Rome*, p. 45.
¹⁰¹ See *Digest* 22.2.6 for a discussion of whether, in such an arrangement where the ship and cargo were lost, the investor could make a claim on the cargoes of the consortium's other ships.

Lenders also took extra steps to reduce the risk of negligence or fraudulence on the part of the trader. This could include having witnesses attest to the cargo being loaded onto the ship. The investor also often sent a representative (supercargo), probably a slave or freedman, on the voyage to keep an eye on the trader. Such risk control could involve making sure the trader took the route specified in the contract and did not practice barratry, whereby his misconduct resulted in damage to the vessel or its cargo. Some investors had a representative stipulated in the contract and had the cost involved ascribed to the trader, but the law placed strict limits on what these charges could be, showing that cheating could be done by both parties to the deal.

4. Balancing risk and reward. It was possible to finance seaborne trade by means of ordinary loans, and in such cases the rate of interest would be capped at 12 per cent and the trader would still have to repay the loan even if the ship sank. It is interesting to consider why both sides might have preferred to enter into a maritime loan agreement instead. In effect, the maritime structure offered a means for both lender and borrower to tailor their financial exposure according to their risk appetite. For the investor, the removal of the interest rate cap offered a means of generating higher returns. Their experience would tell them that the risk premium on such lending was generous and so, over the long term, could be expected to produce a high return even if some ships would be lost. Given that most investors in maritime loans were by definition wealthy, we can see that they were in a position to cope with this extra risk because the loan represented a manageable part of their total assets. By contrast, for the trader, who might own only one ship or was in any case highly likely to be much less wealthy than the investor, transferring the downside risk of the cargo being lost was worth the higher level of financing cost. If the ship sank, the trader still had to bear the loss of the ship, but at least he did not have to repay the loan for the cargo, which, it is important to remember, could have a value several times that of the vessel. For both parties, the nature of the proposed venture would also have affected their own perception of the risks involved, but clearly the two parties to the deal would have had fundamentally different attitudes to risk.

5. Insurance against risk. To some extent it is possible to see maritime loans as providing an element of insurance. The loan served to transfer the risk of cargo loss from the trader to the investor. The investor (insurer) was compensated for taking on this extra risk by receiving a higher level of interest, and, even though this was not in the form of an insurance

premium, the effect was a similar transfer of money.[102] Where the loan did not provide insurance was, of course, for any loss of the boat (a type of insurance known as bottomry). Insurance is also based on a calculation of expected loss rates relative to the size of premia. It is therefore collective, in that it insures against a wide number of individual risks and involves the payment of a capital sum in the event of loss. The insurance premium represents a specific price for a third party to assume a specific risk. None of this was present in the maritime loan, which can be seen more as an aleatory contract between individuals. When the emperor Claudius, during a food shortage, decided to underwrite all the storm-related losses of merchants in order to improve the supply of grain, this was a crisis measure and did not involve either any premium payment or calculation of the potential liability. It was an action that had to be done for political purposes, and the emperor was not worried about the possible cost.[103] The purpose of the maritime loan was to provide a sufficiently high return to entice wealthy individuals to finance the risky business of commercial trade. Its main aim, in that sense, was to generate working capital. The quid pro quo for the trader was to have some reduction in his own risk, and this element of insurance was therefore embedded in the structure of the loan.

Maritime loans represented a practical legal solution to managing the various risks associated with seaborne commerce. Containing elements of equity, partnership, debt, insurance and even optionality on future profits, they reveal both the relative sophistication of Roman thinking in this area and also its shortcomings. The risks were never calculated in the way that underpins modern investment and insurance, but that does not mean the Romans failed to understand many of the issues involved in practice. Again, the expression of this understanding was not in theoretical but in pragmatic terms.

Annuities and Mortality Risk
A final financial subject to consider is the legal passage known as Ulpian's Table. This is a notoriously difficult text, which has provoked considerable

---

[102] N. Morley, *Trade in Classical Antiquity*, Cambridge: Cambridge University Press, 2007. On the differences between modern marine insurance and maritime loans, see H. E. Anderson, III, 'Risk, shipping, and Roman law,' *Tulane Maritime Law Journal*, 34 (2009), 183–210, pp. 185–6 and 204–5.
[103] Suetonius, *Claudius* 18.

debate, but the aim here is to isolate what level of understanding it reveals about risk.[104]

The background to the table is the previously mentioned Falcidian law of 41 BCE, which stipulated that the legal heir had to receive at least a quarter of the value of an estate, while other beneficiaries could inherit up to three-quarters. These inheritances could come in the form of cash, land, property, usufructs and either fixed-term or life annuities. For the value of the estate to be calculated, it was necessary to calculate the value of any annuities that had been bequeathed in the will. An even more pressing legal issue was that inheritances were taxed at 5 per cent and the table is presented during a discussion of this tax. The jurist Ulpian, in c. 220 CE, therefore provided a table that could be used for such a calculation. Its influence was such that the Tuscan government was still using it to value life annuities in 1814, even though an actuarial calculation had been worked out in the late seventeenth century.

The table lists two factors. The first is the age of the beneficiary, the second is a number that should be used to multiply the size of the annuity to compute the figure for the calculation of the tax liability. It is unclear exactly what this second number represents, and a number of interpretations have been proposed:

1. The first is that it is a simple life expectancy figure. So, according to the table, anyone under the age of twenty in receipt of an annuity bequest should multiply its value by a factor of thirty because that represents how much longer they can be expected to live. There are two problems with this: the first, most importantly, is that it seems to underestimate significantly average life expectancy, implying a life

---

[104] See J. E. Ciecka, 'Ulpian's table and the value of life annuities and usufructs', *Journal of Legal Economics*, 19 (2012), 7–15. On the long-running debate, see M. Greenwood, 'A statistical Mare's Nest?', *Journal of the Royal Statistical Society*, 103 (1940), 246–8; B. W. Frier, 'Roman life expectancy: Ulpian's evidence', *Harvard Studies in Classical Philology*, 86 (1982), 213–51; B. W. Frier, 'Demography', in A. K. Bowman, P. Garnsey and D. Rathbone (eds), *The Cambridge Ancient History XI: The High Empire, A.D. 70–192*, 2nd edition, Cambridge: Cambridge University Press, 2000, pp. 787–816; K. Hopkins, 'On the probable age structure of the Roman population', *Population Studies*, 20 (1966), 245–64. See also S. Haberman and T. A. Sibbett (eds), *History of Actuarial Science*, vol. 1, London: William Pickering, 1995; A. Hald, *A. History of Probability and Statistics and Their Applications before 1750*, Hoboken, NJ: John Wiley, 2003; G. Poitras, *The Early History of Financial Economics, 1478–1776*, Cheltenham: Edward Elgar, 2000, pp. 187–9; T. de Vries and W. J. Zwalve, 'Roman actuarial science and Ulpian's life expectancy table', in L. de Ligt, E. A. Hemelrijk and H. W. Singor (eds), *Roman Rule and Civic Life: Local and Regional Perspectives*, Leiden: Brill, 2004, pp. 275–97.

expectancy at birth in the low twenties.[105] The more minor issue is that the numbers imply no fall in life expectancy between the ages of 39–50.

2. The second interpretation is that the second number simply changes the lifetime annuity into a fixed-term annuity. Of course, this number may also represent Ulpian's estimate of life expectancy in that he came to a figure of thirty for the under-twenties because he thought that was how long they would live and that was how long a fixed-term annuity in effect represented. This would be in line with the simplest way of valuing annuities, which is to value them according to how many years of interest is represented by the purchase price. So, an annuity of 10 that cost 100 would mean that it took 10 years to recoup the purchase price. The problem here is that it fails to take into account the effect of interest, which reduces the present value of the payments. The other difficulty is that there is no evidence that a market existed for fixed-term annuities that would have allowed market rates to be used for the purposes of valuation.[106]

3. The second number represents a maximum value for the calculation of the value of the annuity, the idea being that this would ensure that the legal heir would inherit at least a quarter of the estate by placing a high valuation on any bequests to others. This would also have the effect of maximising the inheritance tax, thereby making this a less attractive way of passing on money and again encouraging the testator to benefit the legal heir.[107] That annuities and usufructs were often left to household members, such as slaves and freedmen, may have made them less socially important than the inheritance to the legal heir and so encouraged their overvaluation.

If it is a table of life expectancies there are problems with it in terms of its demography, for, as Hopkins argued, its structure is so short that it is not 'demographically possible'.[108] It is also not clear on what evidence this second number would have been based. It could have been produced by looking at data from sources such as gravestones or simply generated through intuition, reflecting Ulpian's experience of how long people generally lived. Frier suggests that the formula was probably derived 'from

---

[105] P. Pflaumer, 'Estimations of the Roman life expectancy using Ulpian's Table', *JSM Proceedings, Social Statistics Section*, Alexandria, VA: American Statistical Association, 2666–80.
[106] See Poitras, *The Early History of Financial Economics*, p. 188.
[107] Greenwood, 'A statistical Mare's Nest?'.
[108] See Hopkins, 'On the probable age structure', p. 264 n.32.

a limited use of statistics coupled with some shrewd guesswork'.[109] In terms of risk, however, it is possible to make some observations:

1. The table does show an inverse relationship between age and valuation. In other words, the calculation understands that an annuity is worth less for an older person because they are more likely to live for less time than a younger person. It is, therefore, a mortality table, regardless of which of the earlier interpretations is correct – a table that takes into account probability. While it might be thought that this was fairly obvious, it is noteworthy that the British government was still selling lifelong annuities at the same price regardless of age until the eighteenth century. Presumably, death was sufficiently common at all ages that it was not intuitively obvious that a young person would live longer than someone who had successfully reached maturity.
2. As with other Roman understandings of risk, the table was designed for a practical purpose, namely the legal computation of inheritance tax. It is less interested in theoretical accuracy or complete understanding than in providing a readily available and calculable liability.
3. It makes no allowance for any fluctuations in mortality according to geography, sex or status. This may well have been because the table was intended as a broadly applicable instrument, so that there was no need for any fine-tuning.
4. The table seems to imply that the interest rate is zero, an implication that is acceptable if taking the second number as an equivalent to life expectancy. The present value of an annuity should be calculated using a discount rate equating to the interest rate for loans of that maturity. The seeming lack of discount rate may reflect the fact that, as we saw earlier, the term structure of interest rates was undeveloped and the Romans did not have a clear understanding of the time value of money (that a cash flow in the future needs to be discounted by the interest rate to calculate its present value). It may also reflect a desire to keep the calculation simple. Or it may wish to maximise the taxable sum to ensure that the authorities received their share of the inheritance.

Another interpretation, I suggest, is that the interest rate is effectively incorporated into the second number rather in the same way as the interest

---

[109] Frier, 'Roman life expectancy', pp. 225–6 and 229.

rate on maritime loans reflected both a cost of borrowing and a share of the profits. So, with Ulpian's Table, the multiplying figure could be a life expectancy number discounted by the cost of capital. Long-term annuities are highly sensitive to movements in interest rates. A discount rate of 1 per cent on a thirty-year annuity reduces its present value by approximately 15 per cent. Again, any such discounting in the Roman world was probably not done mathematically or by using an appropriate market interest rate, but by intuition and experience, which broadly understood that future cash flows were not as valuable as near-term ones. If that interpretation is correct, the result is that the second figures look too low when compared with later comparative mortality data, but in practical terms they calculate a fairer tax liability by discounting the life expectancy by an implicit interest rate. This would also mean that Ulpian's estimate of life expectancy was higher than that suggested by the second numbers and more in line with what we might expect. For example, if we assume that a discount rate of 1 per cent was applied, implying a reduction of 15 per cent, then average life expectancy would be increased by 100/85. Given that his figures imply an average life expectancy at birth in the low twenties then an increase of that level would move them more in line with the figure of twenty-five, which is generally accepted as the more accurate figure.[110]

Ulpian's Table cannot thus provide firm evidence for a Roman proto-actuarial approach involving the analysis of mortality data. But it does show an awareness of the principle of the probability of mortality increasing with age and of the need to account for that in financial calculations.[111] The practical application of the table for tax purposes probably suggests why Ulpian felt no need to go further than provide a simple tool with broad application. To start thinking about the theory of probability would have added little practical benefit. Some degree of probabilistic reasoning was what was needed, and so he stopped at that.

An interesting comparison with this kind of intuitive understanding of the risk of death can be gleaned from looking at the charges of burial clubs (*collegia*). If we look at the inscription of the club found at Lanuvium, near Rome, we find that the club had an endowment of 15,000 sesterces yielding 800 per annum, or 5.33 per cent. The entrance fee was 100 sesterces plus a monthly fee of 1.25 sesterces per member (15 sesterces per

---

[110] Pflaumer, 'Estimations of the Roman life expectancy'.
[111] O. B. Sheynin, 'On the prehistory of the theory of probability', *Archive for History of Exact Sciences*, 12 (1974), 97–141.

year). On death, the club paid 300 sesterces to provide for the cost of the funeral. There are various club rules regarding costs of meals and fines but I shall ignore these and focus on the cash flow relating to membership and its associated benefits.

If we assume the club had 100 members, then its income totalled 2,300 (= 800 + (15 × 100)). If ten members died, then it had outflows of 3,000 but could accept 10 new members bringing in 1,000 in joining fees. In other words, it made a small profit of 300 sesterces. If fifteen died, then the club made a loss of 700 sesterces – equivalent to almost all its endowment income. However, the club also had to pay for meals, and this seems to be linked directly to the endowment. So, if we exclude the endowment income of 800 sesterces, then the breakeven rate for the club was between seven and eight deaths (8 deaths would mean income of 1,500 monthly fees + 800 joining fees = 2,300 less 2,400 in funeral payouts = 100 sesterces loss; 7 deaths = 1,500 + 700 − 2,100 = 100 sesterces profit). So the basic cost structure was built on the premise that under 10 per cent of the membership would die per annum on average. If we compare this with the life expectancy suggested by modern data, the Model West life expectancy table suggests that 10 per cent of thirty-year-old males and 8.7 per cent of twenty-five-year-old males will die each year. We do not know the average age of the club members, but it is plausible that the high level of mortality and the social benefits of belonging would have encouraged people to join relatively young. The conclusion is that, in broad terms, the fee structure implicitly accounts for the risk of death in the membership in a way that is not dramatically out of line with mortality levels from later data. Whether there was any level of calculation or data collection behind this cost structure is impossible to say, and it may simply reflect a simple assessment based on past experience and what seemed intuitively sensible. None of this was sophisticated by modern standards, but it does suggest an appreciation of the mortality risks individuals faced, at the same time as attempting to limit corporate exposure to them.

Religion

A final area I wish to examine is religion. We saw in Chapter 3 how the Romans tried to understand and cope with the uncertainties of the future by means of various religious ideas and how they consulted a range of religious experts in order to obtain guidance on how to act.[112]

---

[112] On defining divination, see Beerden, *Worlds Full of Signs*, pp. 19–42.

The Romans' longstanding rituals were used to manage relations between humans and the gods and encourage them to deliver benefits to their mortal worshippers. But they also innovated in the religious sphere, as well as incorporating new religious practices from outside. Here I look at what their religious practices can tell us about Romans' attitudes to risk and their perceptions of the uncertainties of the future. Rather than displaying a different approach to the more rational areas of risk management that we have seen already in this chapter, we will see that Roman religious developments employed similar levels of probabilistic thinking.

Dice Oracles

Various aleatory practices in a religious context were used to discern divine guidance and to help the individual decide on a particular course of action. Dice and knucklebone oracles seem to have been widely known. The oracle in the town of Kremna, one of the towns in Pisidia mentioned earlier, had a statue of Mercury, the god of trade and profit, on top of its column, a suitable god for a place of business. Many of the replies relate to Mercury's specialities, suggesting that the pillar was often consulted by small businessmen and traders embarking on travel. The answers display a number of attitudes relating to risk:

1. There is a sense of risk-aversion in the replies, reflected in a keenness to avoid confrontation ('by avoiding hostility and ill-feeling you will eventually reach the prizes') and to avoid the law ('it is terrible to enter into a quarrel and a judicial lawsuit').
2. Uncertainty generated anxiety and the answers often seek to reduce the enquirer's stress, with phrases such as 'do not distress yourself', 'stay calm' and 'don't be afraid'.
3. The imagery within the text often highlights the futility of certain courses of action ('you are looking for a fish in the ocean') as well as the potential dangers ('do not place your hand in the mouth of a wolf', 'a great fiery lion wanders about'). Rural imagery such as this personified the risks facing an individual into forms they could more easily comprehend, in a way comparable to the animals of Aesop's fables and proverbs.
4. The replies have a bias towards positive outcomes. Approximately 70 per cent are positive and 18 per cent negative, with 12 per cent recommending delay. What is not clear is whether these positive answers are weighted towards those throws of the knucklebones which

are more likely to occur because of the unequal probability of each side landing (the two flat sides are four times more likely to occur than the two narrow sides). There is evidently no precise correlation between the positivity of the outcome and the frequency of throws. Ehmig has found some broad trends in that the answers relating to business and travel are weighted towards the middle of the frequency range, with more extreme negative events being more likely to be located on the less probable throws.[113] But this does not mean that there is any understanding of the probabilities involved.

5. The range of possibilities is limited to the fifty-six throws, reflecting a world where there was a limited range of outcomes. Even if the uncertainty level about which outcome would occur was high, the range of uncertainties was not.
6. The location of these advice columns in the forum suggests a conceptual link between business and other aleatory activities. Business involved taking risks and the outcomes were uncertain but the rewards potentially high.
7. The appearance of other non-business risks, such as illness and death, suggest that a similar conceptual parallel was drawn between life risks and chance, but the religious context emphasises that the outcome was not random but could be affected by human actions to influence the divine.

The Oracles of Astrampsychus

At this point I want to revisit a similar set of oracles, the Oracles of Astrampsychus.[114] They date from the second century CE and consist of a list of ninety-two questions that it was possible for the questioner to put to the gods. The oracles were extremely popular for centuries: ten copies were found in the rubbish dumps of Egypt alone.[115] A later, Christianised version was also produced. Unlike the dice oracles, these are very confusing to use, in fact deliberately so in order to enhance the reputation of the diviner who was being consulted. Each question has ten different possible responses, and the questioner would either choose a number between one

---

[113] See Ehmig, 'Antiker Umgang mit Wahrscheinlichem'.
[114] Toner, *Popular Culture in Ancient Rome*, pp. 46–52.
[115] The oracles can be found in translation in Hansen, *Anthology of Ancient Greek Popular Literature*. See also Klingshirn, 'Christian divination in late Roman Gaul'.

and ten or select a number by drawing a lot or by rolling a ten-sided dice, meaning that, unlike in the case of knucklebones, the outcomes were equally probable. To make matters even more confusing, there are also eleven dummy decades of responses to questions that do not exist. They are, as Hansen says, 'easy to use but difficult to fathom'.[116] The topics addressed are mainly practical. The questions are cross-societal, ranging from those of slaves, 'am I going to be sold', to the ambitious, presumably free citizen, 'will I become a senator?' They are unsentimental and pragmatic, and, as Klingshirn says of the later *sortes sangallenses*, 'for the most part, it warns clients to look out for their own good fortune, to make decisions on the basis of aggressive self-interest'.[117]

For each question, the ten possible answers are spread throughout the text with what appears to be a balance between positive and negative responses, but on closer inspection they reveal an awareness of the underlying risks relating to certain questions. To question thirty (Q30), for example, 'will I rear the baby?', the answers reflect the risks relating to child rearing in Roman society. Of the ten possible answers, three are 'survive', three 'survive with toil', two 'die', one 'not reared', one 'thrives'. This is not a balanced set of replies. Two infants die, one is abandoned, and three have health problems. It also implies probabilities about each of these events happening. It suggests there was only a 10 per cent chance that the baby would thrive but a 20 per cent chance that it would die. Comparative evidence suggests that about 25 per cent of all Roman children would have died in their first year. This compares with 20 per cent in the implied figures, which also suggests that 30 per cent survive only 'with toil'. This suggests that the probabilities are not significantly different from the underlying social reality. It also suggests that the reason the Oracles of Astrampsychus were so popular over such a long period of time was because they broadly reflected the realities of Roman life. Clearly, any one individual questioner will get a one-in-ten answer, but over the centuries consultants will have formed the conclusion that the oracles were useful because they reflected the various possible outcomes of life, and hence might be helpful in making life-changing decisions.

The range of possible answers to other questions reveals a similar level of awareness of the background risks Romans faced. When Q64 asks, 'am I going to see a death?'; no fewer than seven responses say 'yes'. Partly this is because death was so ubiquitous, but, presuming that the question refers to a

---

[116] Hansen, *Anthology of Ancient Greek Popular Literature*, p. 289.
[117] Klingshirn, 'Christian divination in late Roman Gaul', p. 112.

specific incidence of illness, it reflects the fact that the questioner would be asking only if the sick person was already seriously ill, and in the ancient world serious illness was likely to be fatal. A similar indication of high mortality rates in the Roman world is that 30 per cent of the replies responding to Q34, 'will I inherit from my mother', are 'no, she'll bury you'.

On travel, Q12, 'will I sail safely?', tells us to expect a 50 per cent chance of delays and a 20 per cent chance of grave danger including shipwreck. Q80, 'is the traveller alive?', tells us that there is a 60 per cent chance of his being fine – 'don't be distressed' – but a 30 per cent likelihood of his being dead (one of the deaths is caused by poisoning). Several questions concern debt. Q25, 'will I be able to borrow money?', has a mixed collection of responses: four are outright negative, which underlines the difficulty in accessing credit in the ancient world. Two of the positive replies emphasise that borrowing was often a face-to-face transaction: 'You will eventually borrow money from the person you wish to' and 'not yet', as 'someone doesn't trust you'. Lenders had to be cultivated in the same way as other wealthy patrons. In Q26 a worried questioner asks, 'will I pay back what I owe?' This yields a fifty-fifty set of responses, implying a 50 per cent default rate, well above the level that implied default rates had earlier suggested. Again, perhaps it is because the questioner is already worried enough to be consulting the gods that makes for such a negative outlook in the responses.

The largest number of questions is about family matters and relationships. We have seen how managing family life was key to controlling risk, which made taking oracular advice a sensible course of action. Q21 asks, 'will I marry and will it be to my advantage?' This was not simply a matter of the heart. Of the ten possible responses, 80 per cent of the responses say the marriage will proceed. Perhaps by the time the questioner has got as far as asking the oracle matters will have progressed too far to be easily stopped. A quarter of the marriages end in divorce, and three more can be termed unhappy arrangements. The social pressure to marry pushed people into marriage even when they obviously had doubts. The responses suggest that many people may well have gone into marriage with low expectations of personal happiness. It was business as much as pleasure.

There are problems with this interpretation, highlighted by three of the questions in particular.[118] The first is, 'am I being poisoned?', to which five answers are positive. The second is, 'will I become a town-councillor?', to

---

[118] See Beard, 'Risk and the humanities; alea iacta est'. Beard argues against what she calls an 'actuarial line' in attempting to discern some traces of a risk agenda and an embodied discourse of risk, which she sees as being 'based on arithmetic probabilities'.

which eight of the answers are positive. Finally, 'is my wife having a baby?', to which all ten replies are affirmative. The high level of positive responses raises a number of interesting issues relating to Roman understandings of risk:

1. It is clear that the oracles display an approach that could be termed probabilistic thinking rather than anything that would fit the kind of narrow definition of risk found in an actuarial calculation, based on the analysis of relevant data. These questions highlight how much more useful it is to think of ideas relating to probability as existing along a spectrum rather than being a hard division between actuarial approaches and all other ways of thinking about uncertainty.
2. The oracular responses claim to date from the distant past, as a means of enhancing their authority, but they were in fact invented, probably in the second century CE. This shows that this kind of innovative probabilistic thinking was being applied not just to areas such as law or logistics but also to religion, a sphere that we might imagine was more dominated by traditional approaches.
3. How the compiler of the oracles formed his ideas is impossible to say. He could have used some basic data, derived from evidence such as tombstones, used intuition or simply made it all up. The third of these seems highly unlikely because of the similarities across the questions, for in that case the answers should be relatively random and display no perceptible relationship to any underlying social reality. The first is possible, but there is no evidence in any other area, even for Ulpian's Table, and the religious context makes it less likely that there was any perceived need for a high level of accuracy. The second option, consisting of intuition, experience and 'gut feeling', is likely to be what informed the range of outcomes in each question. This reliance on intuition means that we should not be surprised if the questions display some inconsistencies.
4. The diviner may also have rigged his answers according to what he could sense from the client about the likely outcome. This would be easily done, especially if the client were illiterate, and probably not hard to do anyway given the complexity of the whole procedure. Eleven questions deal with official posts, ranging from town councillor to clerk in the marketplace to senator. Official posts were a source of status and greater financial security, and people were understandably keen to know if they were going to get the job. The pool of questioners, therefore, was likely to be highly self-selecting and consist of ambitious men in pursuit of a public career. It is not surprising that

the diviner would weight his responses towards the positive, partly reflecting the reality that these were the kinds of individuals who were likely to be successful but also telling his clients what they wanted to hear. The other questions involving offices display a similar bias: Q16, 'will I advance in office?', and Q35, 'will I be an official', both have seven positive replies, with the best answer spelling out what the individuals were looking for: 'you will be esteemed and honoured'. Q88, 'will I become a Senator', also has seven positives, but four answers emphasise that it will take time. By contrast, several questions deal with legal matters but are all equally divided between positive and negative replies. This is not surprising, given that the law would always divide equally between winners and losers. So, while individuals received replies drawn from a range of responses that reflected some awareness of the underlying probabilities that such events would occur, it is also clear that such an awareness was heavily affected by subjective experience.

5. The questions can also be somewhat ambiguous. The question 'is my wife having a baby' translates the more general Greek question 'does my wife bring forth children?' In other words, the English translation puts the emphasis on whether the woman is pregnant, whereas the original Greek replies could simply indicate that she will be productive at some point, although it is the case that the present tense is used. Given Roman women's core role of child rearing, this was a highly likely proposition; so likely that it made no sense to the compiler to even allow not giving birth as a possibility. But when we look more closely at the answers, we infer that the question is not so much about being pregnant as about whether the wife and unborn child will survive the dangers of childbirth, which was always a risky process in the ancient world. Four say the birth will be 'with danger', one more 'to the point of death'. One woman will give birth to a girl 'who won't live long'. One infant 'will survive', one other 'will do well', while two say 'you will father a baby but it will be unprofitable', which says something of the paternal attitude to children.

6. The replies then do not just provide a simple mirror of the underlying reality. They also reflect the social tensions and anxieties that living in the ancient world generated. The question 'have I been poisoned', to which five of the replies give a positive answer, reflects a world where sickness was frequent, food hygiene was poor and stomach illnesses in particular were therefore commonplace, but people had little medical understanding of what caused any of these ailments. Given the socially

competitive world they inhabited, their first response was to point the finger at others and suspect foul play. The negative answers are also interesting in this regard as two state, 'but you have been bewitched', suggesting that hostile spells were also seen as a likely cause of such illness. Only one answer seeks to downplay this sense of social hostility by asking the questioner, 'why are you being irrational?'

Dream Interpretation

I want to finish this section by seeing whether it is possible to discern ancient expectations about the future from another area of religious practice, namely dream interpretation. Artemidorus' five books on the subject include three that are mainly theoretical, and seek to analyse every possible outcome, a fourth which is more practical and explains new ways of interpreting ambiguous points, and a fifth which is a compilation of ninety-five examples from his own experience, which he feels are reliable and useful. It is this fifth book I want to focus on, since it is unstructured and so can be taken as representing a reasonable cross-section of scenarios. The treatise was written as a private manual for his son, whom he advises not to reveal the contents. I want to show that we can use this book to learn something of the way the Romans looked at future dangers and what they understood about the likelihood of these happening.

To do this, I give each outcome a simple score according to whether its scenario was very bad (−2), bad (−1), neutral (0), good (+1) or very good (+2). The totals are as follows:

(−2) 55
(−1) 16
(0) 7
(+1) 6
(+2) 11

Obviously, there is a subjective element to this scoring, but one of the advantages of focusing on Book Five is that is considerably more straightforward in its interpretations than the earlier books. Using the same scale, I then scored the content of the preceding dreams:

(−2) 9
(−1) 39
(0) 40

(+1) 6
(+2) 1

Comparing the two sets of scores, we can see that sixty-one situations showed a deterioration from the dream to the actual outcome, nineteen were neutral, mixed or unclear, while fifteen improved. Fourteen dreams were seemingly good or bad but turned out to predict the opposite. No dreams went from (−2) to (−1) and only two moved from (+1) to (+2). By far the largest group was the fifty-four that turned from (0) or (−1) to (−2). A neutral or random set of interpretations would have given a more even spread of movements. The actual spread of the interpretations suggests that there was a strong bias towards having negative expectations about future events.

The degree of that negative bias is revealed when we look at how many digits the outcome relative to the dream moved by (from −2 to 1 counts as an improvement of 3). Twelve improved by two, three or four ranks, three improved by one rank, ten were unchanged, but twenty-seven deteriorated by one rank and thirty-four by two, three or four ranks. We can conclude the following:

1. From the dream interpreter's perspective, it made sense to predict bad news. His clients feared the worst and expected it, too. There was no sense that things would work out well in the end; in fact, quite the opposite. This may explain why the outcomes of the dice oracles noted earlier were more positive: people had such low expectations that matters rarely turned out as badly as they imagined.
2. There may well be a self-selecting bias here in that individuals were more likely to consult an interpreter when they had some underlying cause for anxiety. This underlying cause might have resulted in what we would term 'anxiety dreams' and may also have fed through into more negative outcomes in reality.
3. What appear as minor negatives in dreams are often portrayed as being magnified in real life. There was an expectation that life would throw up regular difficulties and that these were likely to increase in difficulty over time. Whether this was pessimism or realism is impossible to say.
4. It is noticeable that a number of the dreams deal with high-impact events of very low probability, such as finding treasure or accidentally committing incest. Their frequency of appearance does not seem to be out of kilter with what we would expect from a normal distribution of outcomes but clearly these extremes say something about what Romans

thought about 'living the dream' or, conversely, what constituted their 'worst nightmares'.

Constructing Resilience

We saw in Chapter 3 how Rome's risk culture encouraged certain personality traits in its members, whether from the elite or the lower orders. I want to conclude by looking briefly at how attitudes to risk were also central to the conscious construction of identity, particularly among the elite by means of an interest in Stoic philosophy.

Horace's exhortation held that admiring nothing was key to being able to adopt an attitude towards life that would make the individual undisturbed by fear in the face of danger (*Letters* 1.6). Those who admire and desire riches, power and luxury, he argues, are terrified of being afflicted by unforeseen events, whereas true peace of mind comes from being indifferent to what the future might bring. This was a Stoic ideal, of apathy (apatheia), that represented the repression of all personal emotion. It is an attitude that we can perhaps see best for these purposes in the emperor Marcus Aurelius' *Meditations*. Written as a kind of personal self-improvement manual, they record his notes to self about how best to cope with the many difficulties that came his way. These problems included the significant dangers he faced while on his extensive periods of campaigning, and it is clear that many of the entries were written during active military service.

Such Stoic ideas were not peculiar to Marcus. He had been educated in Stoicism having been adopted by the emperor Antoninus Pius, the aim being to inculcate in the youth what might today be termed a 'resilient' personality. Unfazed by danger, able to control both anger and his passions, and untainted by a desire for the trappings of wealth, the future emperor acquired through his education the mental strength to deal with the huge pressures and almost unlimited temptations that would face him once in office. The list of problems that confronted him during his reign would have overwhelmed a less capable or well-prepared individual. War in the east and a coalition of powerful northern tribes threatened the stability of the empire. The Antonine Plague decimated the population and deprived him of much-needed manpower for his military expeditions. Major floods in Rome destroyed substantial stocks of grain, resulting in hunger among the general populace. The size of the threat posed in the north is reflected in the fact that Marcus was to spend almost all of his reign campaigning in that region, as well as confronting a significant revolt from the commander of the eastern legions, Avidius Cassius.

Resilient is almost too weak a word for Marcus' ideal personality type: 'Be like the promontory against which the waves continually break, but it stands firm and tames the fury of the water around it.'[119] Death held no fear for him: 'Think continually... how many heroes are dead after killing thousands, and how many tyrants who have used their power over men's lives with terrible insolence, as if they were immortal.' All human affairs are deemed to be 'ephemeral and worthless' and the best attitude individuals can adopt is to see themselves as akin to olives that fall off the tree when ripe, content that they have experienced such life as they had. Whatever misfortunes happen, the individual should carry on, 'free from pain, neither crushed by the present nor fearing the future', and in this way be able to cope better with the situation than those who do not adhere to Stoic principles and so are traumatised by what has afflicted them. Whenever, therefore, the individual is faced with an anxiety-inducing situation, the key, says Marcus, is not to see it as a misfortune but to have the strength of personality to be able to bear it in a dignified fashion.

The widespread interest in philosophy among the Roman elite developed much earlier, during the republic, and can in part be interpreted as a consolation for their loss of political power with the advent of military strongmen, such as Julius Caesar, and the later emperors. But its attraction can also be explained by the resources it offered for dealing with unexpected calamity. Personal happiness was constructed as something that would come from managing down expectations concerning the future, while simultaneously developing a psychological resilience in the face of the inevitable troubles that life would send. Marcus Aurelius was a high-profile example of this kind of personal development but it is also found in many other philosophical texts, such as the work of Epictetus. Unlike the more cultural forms of personal development we encountered in Chapter 3, the philosophical musings of Marcus reflect an approach of ongoing critical self-examination in line with Stoic principles as he perceived them. The emperor not only strove to behave in line with these principles but also worked continuously both to hone his understanding of them and to forge his own personality accordingly.

Conclusion

It was only in the seventeenth century that people began to think about probability in a mathematical way. This chapter has argued that the

---

[119] 4.48–9, trans. G. Long.

Romans thought about the probable in a variety of other ways: practical, legal, financial and religious. All of this exhibited a degree of probabilistic thinking, some of which was taken to a high level of sophistication. If we see thinking about probability as existing on a spectrum, then the Romans displayed plenty of active and rational consideration of ideas of uncertainty and future danger. It would be wrong to overemphasise the divide between this and the more culturally determined attitudes that we examined in Chapter 3 as part of the 'risk culture', since many of these more traditional attitudes allowed for a level of interpretation and conscious calculation at the level of practical application. But it is apparent that Roman society developed a range of new expert techniques that allowed it to deal with what we would call risk in a sophisticated and practical way.

CHAPTER 5

Moral Hazards
Constructing Risk

The previous chapters have looked at the practical ways in which the Romans dealt with the risks they faced, the ideas they developed to cope with future uncertainty and the relationship between some of their conceptions and the underlying dangers themselves. I have argued throughout that the Romans had an awareness of probability, albeit not one that was developed in a statistical way, and that they clearly understood the anxieties generated by uncertainty. But anxieties do not simply reflect the underlying dangers. Fear is itself created by society's debates about what count as risks and how these should be managed. What of modernity? Beck has argued that modernity's uncertainties have arisen from technological developments themselves, in that these have generated self-destructive threats that they are incapable of controlling. Modernity in his view is not only reflexive about its own technological advances, it has become self-confrontational. Modernity has seen many of the old certainties of traditional roles break down in the face of rapid social change and replaced them with self-doubt and angst. In this chapter, I argue that Rome's social structure generated its own specific set of anxieties. Just as technology has today created anxieties about the downside of that innovation, in Rome, empire generated a set of fears concerning its perceived negative side effects. These were focused on moral issues and their anxieties were expressed in areas where they had their own expertise, in particular the law and rhetoric. Their fears were also often constructed in a backward-looking way, seeking to reduce future risk by returning to the traditions of the past. As a result, we can see that Roman society established its own unique way of dealing with its particular set of perceived risks that parallels the process of reflexivity that Beck has identified in the modern world.

Beck argues that the risks faced by pre-modern societies were as visible as their causes, but risks of the imagination, such as religious pollution and moral contamination, could neither be seen nor regarded as purely physical threats. Symbolic risks of this kind might seem to be 'unreal' in a sense, but, as Hacking observes, 'if something is treated as real it will be real in its consequences'.[1] Why does a society worry about certain dangers and not others? The term risk is often applied to the potential harm done by certain factors, but deciding what counts as harmful requires notions of good and bad outcomes.[2] It therefore has an inherently moral element, which places a societal value on certain possible events.[3] A narrow definition of risk can be used to look at probable outcomes in a neutral way, such as the roll of a dice. But once risk is used in a broader way to evaluate society's dangers, it is apparent that risk is part of a far wider political vocabulary of moral responsibility and accountability.[4]

These risks are not presented in a neutral manner. A narrative, or discourse, develops around the discussion and treatment of these risks, which serves to locate particular risks in a wider network of moral meaning and a chain reaction of causation. This represents the rhetoric of risk. This broader narrative helps to link certain types of behaviour in the collective mind, and thereby to exaggerate them in order to generate a communal response to the perceived moral threat. It becomes the responsibility of society and its upholders of values to act against such threats to social order. Those individuals whose behaviour or beliefs pose such a threat are themselves labelled as dangerous and culpable, deserving of whatever societal actions are taken against them in a process of blame attribution.[5] The risk-generating individual or group is singled out as an enemy in order to uphold the moral solidarity of the community. What a society counts as a risk, therefore, reflects many of its core structures.[6] Roman society's main characteristics included its hierarchical social order, its conservatism, its military success and its belief that it was the support of the gods, the *pax deorum*, that had led to that success. Anything threatening to destabilise these features generated a powerful moral backlash. What I want to do in this chapter is look at how the Romans dealt with such moral hazards in the areas of religion, luxury and sexual behaviour to show how the Romans constructed their risks by reference to the past. Whereas the modern

---

[1] Hacking, 'Risk and dirt', p. 19.
[2] See esp. Ericson and Doyle, *Risk and Morality*; G. Rigakos and A. Law, 'Risk, realism and the politics of resistance', *Critical Sociology*, 35 (2009), 79–103.
[3] Douglas, 'Risk as a forensic resource', p. 10.   [4] Doyle and Ericson, *Risk and Morality*, p. 4.
[5] Douglas, *Risk and Blame*.
[6] On cultural bias and risk perception, see A. Wildavsky and K. Dake, 'Theories of risk perception: who fears what and why?', *Daedalus*, 119 (1990), 41–60.

approach to risk sees it as a concept that is inherently linked to how we want to see a reformed and improved world in the future, the Roman approach was to see risk as behaviour that deviated from the past. Risk control therefore became a matter of eradicating actions that threatened the pre-existing order, and the future represented a reconstruction rather than a reform of the past.

Religious Risk

Most of the time, the Romans were broadly tolerant of other religions and incorporated many new religious practices into Roman society alongside their conquests of many different peoples. It was only when certain practices were thought to be threatening the support of the gods that a communal response was thought necessary. Hence, if a vestal virgin broke her vow of chastity, she was dressed in burial dress and carried, while still alive, in a kind of mock funeral procession. Accompanied by her family and friends, the vestal was taken on a funeral bier to the Colline Gate where she was interred in an underground cell and left to die in order by her expiation to free the Roman state of religious risk.[7] This was an outlook which interpreted misfortune as evidence of wrongdoing. Unacceptable religious acts were not seen as self-contained acts but rather as assaults on the entire fabric of the community with potentially widespread harmful effects. Unfaithful vestals were often discovered when the sacred eternal flame, which burned in the Temple of Vesta, unexpectedly went out. This much-feared event was read as an omen of imminent disaster. It would itself be seen as a sign from the goddess that one of her attendants had been unfaithful and was therefore threatening to bring harm on the state. The answer was simple: find out which vestal was the guilty party and so eradicate the cause of the divine offence and the threat to the community stemming from it. So a vestal deemed guilty was duly buried alive, various supplicatory rites were held to appease the goddess and the *pax deorum* was re-established.

We can see this close mental correlation between religion and disastrous events in the various accounts of ancient writers of events such as earthquakes, fires and floods.[8] Roman texts are most interested in what can be

---

[7] Plutarch, *Life of Numa* 10.
[8] R. F. Newbold, 'The reporting of earthquakes, fires and floods by ancient historians', *Proceedings of the African Classical Association*, 16 (1982), 28–36. See Toner, *Roman Disasters*, pp. 110–13.

gleaned from the disaster about the state of relations with the gods. This can take various forms, ranging from descriptions of the divine anger that has caused the event (6 per cent), to the carrying out of expiatory rites (6 per cent) and the consultation of oracles (6 per cent). Of most interest by far are the associated portents accompanying the disaster, which are interpreted so as to emphasise the divine nature of the occurrence (28 per cent). That a variety of strange signs were reported to have occurred at the same time as the disaster was thought to underline the fact that the disaster should be given a religious interpretation and was a manifestation of divine anger at some particular human action. The seriousness with which these divine interpretations were taken is reflected in the fact that a significant number of accounts report that government policy changed as a result of the premonitory disaster, such as the abandonment of a planned invasion (12 per cent). It seemed perfectly reasonable to ascribe positive outcomes in human affairs to divine will. Similarly, misfortune was understood as a scourge sent by the gods to punish Rome for any social or political acts that had hurt divine sensibilities. The persecution of any religious groups whose behaviour was perceived to be upsetting the gods was a natural corollary of these attitudes. The early Christians were a prominent example but many other types of individual, such as magicians, astrologers, Dionysus worshippers, Manichees and, later, Christian heretics, all suffered at the hands of the Roman state. Even so, persecution was not the norm. Rome's pagan religion represented a broad set of religious practices, so there was no intrinsic drive to stamp out religious difference or innovation. It was usually only when the community felt actively threatened, often because it had suffered a disaster of some kind, that persecution followed. It was a simple form of scapegoating that was designed to be a powerful symbolic reaffirmation of traditional morality.

Religious malpractice, as the Romans interpreted it, posed perhaps the ultimate threat to the Roman order, since it threatened to turn the gods away from their side. While broadly tolerant of many new forms of religious expression, anything that threatened the core support of the gods suffered a vigorous response. The Romans brought to bear their own form of religious expertise to interpret what counted as unacceptable behaviour and what measures should be enacted to ensure both that the religious pollution was extirpated and that the peace of the gods was maintained. From a modern perspective, we might find it hard to see this as 'expertise', but the Romans devoted considerable resources to interpreting divine signals and appeasing any inferred negative sentiments.

The Risk of Luxury

Luxury was never seen as a simple index of increased wealth and imperial success. Rather, it raised all manner of moral anxieties among Rome's ruling classes.[9] Rome's conquest of the Mediterranean resulted in a significant increase in the availability of luxury goods, especially once the occupation of Egypt opened up direct shipping lanes from the Red Sea to Arabia, East Africa and India. These gave access to goods that were, by Roman standards, exotic in the extreme, including silks from China, incenses from Arabia and spices from India.[10] Luxury could serve to reinforce the social order, in that luxury items offered an easy way for individuals to display their status. But the importation of luxury goods also underlined to the Romans how much they had changed from their plainer ancestors and made clear the risks of that change. Roman writers frequently harked back to a golden age when Rome's values were supposedly uncorrupted and simple.[11]

Anxieties relating to luxury partly reflected a belief that the body of male citizens, who had won the empire through its legendary military toughness, was likely to grow soft if it was exposed to the pleasurable effects of the many luxuries Rome now offered. The popularity of bathing was of particular concern, since it seemed obvious that regular soaking in hot water would soften the flesh. The kind of man who bathed daily, dined on delicacies and composed fine verses was hardly likely to make much of a soldier. It was the city of Rome itself that seemed to many elite writers to pose the greatest risk. Rome was where the masses could live off state subsidies and wasted their days at the games given by the emperor. Urban luxury turned the bodies of young men 'so flabby and enervated that death seems likely to make no change in them'.[12]

War exacerbated these fears. Fancy foods, feather beds and sheer silk could have only a negative impact on military discipline. During the conflicts with Carthage in the second century BCE, Scipio the Younger arrived at one camp only to find all manner of licentiousness and luxury.

---

[9] On decadence and sumptuary legislation, see J. Toner, 'Decadence in ancient Rome', in J. Desmarais and D. Weir (eds), *Decadence and Literature*, Cambridge: Cambridge University Press, 2019, pp. 15–29.
[10] A. Wallace-Hadrill, 'The senses in the market-place: the luxury market and eastern trade in imperial Rome', in J. Toner (ed.), *A Cultural History of the Senses in Antiquity*, London: Routledge, 2014, pp. 69–89.
[11] See, for example, Livy 39.6 and Pliny, *Natural History* 9.58.117–18.
[12] Columella *On Agriculture* 1 preface 17.

This, he believed, could only ever result in disorder among the troops. He issued orders for all the soothsayers and prostitutes to be driven out of the camp. He even commanded that the only utensils a soldier should be allowed to possess were a pot, a fork and an earthenware drinking-cup. He banned bathing and said that men should only rub themselves down, not receive massages from others. The troops were forbidden from reclining at dinner, which he ordered should consist only of bread, porridge or boiled meat. The only luxury he allowed the men was that each could keep a silver tankard of not more than two pounds in weight if they so wished. He himself went about wearing a plain black cloak, saying that he was in mourning for the army's lost honour. Luxury posed a moral threat that needed to be addressed if Rome's success was to continue.

Wealth also generated concerns in that it seemed to encourage a shift away from traditional simplicity towards pleasure. As Cato the Elder had said, 'how can a city continue to exist in security when a highly-prized fish is selling for more than an ox?' The moralist Seneca complained that people in Rome now had so much money that they cooled their wine with snow and ate fresh oysters.[13] Expensive spices and perfumes were associated with the supposedly decadent Greek and Persian East, which added to their connotations of immorality. Seneca contrasts the austerity of the Romans of old with his contemporaries' full-length gold mirrors, when 'luxury, encouraged by sheer opulence, has gradually developed for the worst, and vices have taken on enormous growth', even 'amongst soldiers'.[14] It was a concern that made the satirist, Juvenal, take a moral stand. When he saw a 'slave from Canopus' who was now so rich that he was wearing a Tyrian purple cloak and could barely cope with the weight of his gem-encrusted gold rings, it was then 'hard not to write satire'.[15] An older literary form, satire, had to be recreated to cope with a world that was literally satiated with luxury. Anxieties about luxury also had, like most things in ancient Rome, a religious side. Faced with the multiple temptations that empire brought, many Romans worried that their society was slipping into a hubristic quagmire of disgraceful behaviour, which could result in only one thing – the loss of the support of the gods. Luxury, therefore, was believed to pose a very potent threat to Roman security.

Developing Roman legal expertise was directed against the danger posed by luxury. The Roman state enacted sumptuary laws – laws made for the purpose of limiting or preventing expenditure on certain items of personal

---

[13] Seneca, *Moral Letters* 78.23.   [14] Seneca, *Natural Questions* 1.17.7–10.
[15] Juvenal, *Satire* 1.24–5.

consumption, especially luxury items. The second-century CE writer Aulus Gellius, in his discussion of these laws, notes how they were introduced to maintain the frugality of the early Romans.[16] One of the earliest of these was a decree of the Senate concerning the annual Megalensian games, which ordered all the leading citizens to swear an oath before the consuls that they would not spend on dinner more than 120 asses in addition to vegetables, bread and wine, nor would they serve any foreign wine, nor use more than 100 pounds' weight of silverware at the table. What is clear here is how the measures were originally targeted at those at the top of Roman society. The fear was that society would rot from the top if these leaders were corrupted. It also shows the high level of concern regarding the weakening effect of anything perceived to be luxurious overconsumption. The law therefore reflected the authorities' concern about the impact of what was seen as immoral behaviour upon the wider community. Losing the support of the gods because of the immoral behaviour of certain individuals meant that what to us looks like victimless crime risked, from the Roman point of view, bringing disaster down on everyone's heads.[17]

A steady stream of such laws was passed. The Licinian law, probably passed in 103 BCE, limited the financial outlay on designated holiday feasts, while permitting larger sums for weddings. It allowed for a fixed weight of dried meat and other preserved products to be served, but permitted unlimited use of anything grown in the earth, on a vine or in an orchard. Morally acceptable food was that produced naturally from the ground and eaten fresh rather than anything salted, or indeed any kind of meat. Meat was a valuable commodity and best reserved as an offering to the gods. But, as Gellius sadly notes, these laws were soon forgotten, and many wealthy men were gourmandising and 'recklessly pouring their family fortune into an abyss of banquets'. Finally, he lists the Julian law of the emperor Augustus, which limited expenditure on dining to 200 sesterces on a working day, 300 on holidays, and 1,000 at weddings and banquets, and another edict that increased the holiday limit from 300 to 2,000, which itself indicates both the high level of dinner party inflation and the ineffectiveness of the legislation.

Sumptuary laws attempted to regulate more than just the consumption of food and wine. In the aftermath of the crushing defeat at Cannae in 216 BCE, when the Romans lost 50,000 men in a single day and found

---

[16] *Attic Nights* 2.24.
[17] See E. Zanda, *Fighting Hydra-Like Luxury: Sumptuary Regulation in the Roman Republic*, London: Bloomsbury Academic, 2013.

themselves facing defeat at the hands of Hannibal, one of the Roman responses was an attempt to place legal limits on the amount of jewellery and on what colour clothing a woman could wear and how far she could travel in a horse-drawn carriage. When the Roman men had failed to win on the battlefield, a natural response was to blame the women back home. It was as if the women of the household were somehow at fault for having softened their male offspring by wearing too much finery. Again, we see a direct relationship in the Roman mind between personal consumption and military prowess. What was different this time was the attempt to use legislation to put a stop to it, thereby employing a developing area of Roman expertise against what seemed a new type of risk to society.

As the empire grew, luxury became not only an elite matter. We find an increasing concern from the Roman state about the behaviour of the lower classes in certain areas. Taverns, above all, became the focus of a range of laws aimed at limiting the spread of luxury downwards to the ordinary people, even though we might see such establishments as offering luxury of only a very limited kind. Taverns featured prominently in the daily life of the people of Rome, serving as mini leisure centres and, since most people did not have access to cooking facilities, as places to get hot food. Often they also offered other entertainments, including music, prostitution and gambling, even though this was illegal. But where ordinary people found food and fun, the Roman elite saw a risk to their moral health and to social order. In part, taverns represented what the elite saw as the decline of the Roman people from the citizen body that had supplied the manpower for the legions. As Juvenal bemoaned, the Roman people had gone from voting on weighty matters of state to being obsessed with only two things: bread and circuses.[18] Various emperors, therefore, issued sumptuary laws concerning what could be sold in taverns. All of this legislation was driven by the fear that in the sprawling imperial city of Rome it was now not just the upper classes that were enjoying luxury; it was even filtering down to the plebs. And just as the Oppian Law had sought to restrain the personal consumption of women, so laws against taverns and gambling attempted to set limits on what was considered appropriate for an average Roman to consume.

Roman laws on luxury reflected a range of moral concerns: fear of a loss of military strength, fear that luxury was an addiction that would lead to ever greater consumption and fear that lavish expenditure would erode the

---

[18] On taverns, see Toner, *Popular Culture in Ancient Rome*, pp. 109–11.

family fortunes of Rome's aristocratic class. The laws represented an attempt at self-regulation by Rome's elite to prevent luxury from corrupting the ruling class and so undermining the social order, but they also sought to stem any downward flow of that corruption towards the lower orders.

Augustus' Adultery Laws

The transition from republic to empire at the turn of the first century BCE saw a profound shift in the nature of Roman political and public life. The first emperor, Augustus, was faced with unifying a society fractured by decades of civil war. He sought to recreate a unified Roman identity based on traditional themes of piety, virtue and loyalty. The emperor himself was represented as the epitome of these values and served as the cultural centre-point for Roman society as a whole. Luxury, in the form of lavish games, now became the means by which he sought to put this new identity most clearly on view. Pleasure and politics were fused into a powerful alloy which overcame traditional objections to the non-elite having access to leisure and luxury. The games were not thought to corrupt the people because they established imperial legitimacy, maintained social hierarchy and created social consensus. The new political ideology sought to contrast itself with the chaos of the previous republic. Luxury was shorn of some of its decadent connotations as a way of emphasising the revitalisation of Roman society. It was as if the previous chaos of the late republic had itself reflected the lack of control of excessive consumption. The emperors could not argue that they were reducing luxury, and it would have been unpopular to do so, but they could show that luxury was now being put towards a positive moral-political purpose. The previous turbulence was presented as almost a necessary stage for Roman society to have passed through before it could undergo a profound moral rebirth.[19]

Augustus did not want to be seen as an innovator. He wanted to be seen to have 'restored the republic' (*respublica restituta*). Alongside this political rebirth, he wanted to portray his rule as re-establishing the traditional order. We might well see this as political spin designed to camouflage the reality of the autocracy of his rule, but establishing controls on dangerous personal behaviour was a cornerstone of his claim to legitimacy. Sumptuary laws, therefore, received a new articulation under Augustus,

---

[19] See N. Morley, 'Decadence as a theory of history', *New Literary History*, 35 (2004), 573–85.

which was designed to limit the public risk posed by certain kinds of what we would see as private behaviour. His moral laws made adultery for the first time a public, criminal offence. The law now required a husband to prosecute his wife if he discovered her having an affair, otherwise he risked being charged as a pimp. If convicted, the wife had to be immediately divorced. Under the terms of the law, a father could kill his daughter and her lover, provided that he caught them in the act, that they were having sex either in his own house or in that of his son-in-law, and that he killed them both immediately. Adultery, as so legally defined, did not apply to all, since it depended upon the woman's status. Married men could commit adultery only with respectable married women. A wife committed adultery if she slept with any other man, even a slave. By contrast, it was impossible for a female slave or prostitute to commit adultery. The bias against women reflects the wider patriarchal culture and the specific anxieties of a male elite, who constructed the female body as being 'at risk' and so in need of government and control. As an indication of how seriously Augustus took these laws, if an accusation went to court, slaves were exceptionally permitted to give evidence against their masters and mistresses.

In introducing these laws against what was regarded as immoral sexual behaviour, Augustus was making a determined effort to reinforce the sanctity of marriage as an institution and the integrity of the family home. After two generations of civil strife during the collapse of the republic, his moral laws acted as a core part of the first emperor's attempt to reinstate order to all aspects of the Roman world. In this view, political chaos had been a reflection of moral chaos, which had itself been revealed in a range of risky individual behaviours, whether in terms of consumption of luxuries, greed, violence or sex. As with the sumptuary legislation, much of this can be seen as a symbolic attempt to restore order. Some openly flouted the legislation, including Augustus' own daughter, Julia, who was banished to an island.[20] The poet Ovid's *The Art of Love* (*Ars amatoria*), a textbook on how to conduct a love affair, shows that elite authors could also delight in subverting the official position. That this blatant subversion of Augustus' attempts at moral reform probably contributed to his being later exiled to the miserable Black Sea town of Tomis shows how seriously the emperor took these reforms, even if they did contain a significant symbolic element.

---

[20] Suetonius, *Augustus* 65.

That contemporary morality was an issue for the Romans of this time is clear from the opening of Livy's *ab Urbe Condita*. He states that he has no interest in Rome's mythical past or whether the Roman people's father was none other than Mars.[21] What interested Livy was 'life and morals', the ways in which empire was won by Rome's heroes, then the process by which, 'with the gradual relaxation of discipline, morals first gave way, as it were, then sank lower and lower, and finally began the downward plunge which has brought us to the present time, when we can endure neither our vices nor their cure'. Livy's emphasis on Rome's heroes of the past showed how 'wholesome and profitable' the study of history was, in that it made clear the principal lesson that would arrest Rome's decline: that Augustus was a modern hero cast from a traditional mould. The Romans had suffered in the late republic, a punishment they deserved because of their own immoral behaviour, but history showed the path to a new golden future that represented a restoration of the past.

We can see this as an attempt to create a future where the present was reconciled with the past. This two-way process served to change the Roman understanding of the idea of the past in a way that no hard division seemed applicable between the Augustan present and the Republican tradition. As with a damaged antique, an act of restoration involves adding new material to blend in with the old in order to generate a new appearance of authenticity. In a sense, what is created is the same, in a sense it is not. By using traditional morality, we can see Augustus as freeing the future from the powerful grip of the past by copying it in a way that made it clear that it could not be repeated. Rather than simply trying to appropriate tradition, he emphasised that the past had been both revived and improved upon by allowing those ancient morals to operate within a framework that enabled them to be observed properly.

An Augustan future worked because it set limits on all people's behaviour, even the emperor's and his family. It worked because those limits were flexible and symbolic, rarely needing to be rigorously enforced. Above all, it worked because it restored the political system of the past in a form that meant it could function effectively with Augustus as its enforcer. This imperial settlement developed a sophisticated system of mutually beneficial relationships between the various classes of Rome. Rome's past played a core role in the establishment of the ideology that supported this culture and, in its mutually reconstitutive relationship with the present, sought to establish a more stable future.

---

[21] Livy 1 preface 8–10, Loeb translation.

Whose Risk?

Imperial ideology constructed itself as a safe space, which protected Rome's inhabitants from the various risks that the successful acquisition of empire had exposed them to. By redefining traditional notions of morality, it established a claim to decide on what now counted as dangerous activity. The problem is that it is easy for us to accept this claim and fail to see that legislation itself highlighted that there were competing claims for what counted as risky behaviour. The law gives us a good idea of what mattered to the elite, but we should be careful about extrapolating from that to Roman society as a whole or different groups within it. The reality was more complicated. A closer examination of the context of these laws can show how various groups may well have looked at certain risks very differently.

What, for example, would the ordinary Romans who frequented the numerous taverns have seen as the greatest risks they faced? Access to food would probably have ranked high on their list. The gambling that went on in taverns was seen as harmless fun and an opportunity to make money, and as a way to enhance local reputation. The laws banning such gambling were widely ignored and even mocked in the use of signs composed of witty sayings that represented a gaming board. Legislation against taverns therefore cannot be read as an indicator of social consensus. The opposite was more likely to be the case, with taverns providing ready availability of affordable meals that would probably not have been perceived as luxurious by their consumers, as well as harmless entertainment. The way that narratives were constructed around certain risks, therefore, reflected unresolved conflicts between different social groups. Similarly, the fact that elite-authored texts concerning various disasters focused on the effect on public life reflected the centrality of this to elite life. We should not imagine that the ordinary people who were vulnerable to these disasters would have reported them in the same way or identified the same set of risks as being most important. Their accounts might be expected to focus far more on the communal, familial or individual trauma they had suffered. What we need to do, then, when looking at Roman texts relating to risks is to try to construct a more polyphonic social memory, which takes into account some of these competing attitudes.

Popular attitudes towards risks such as urban fires, for example, seem to have been very different from those of the elite writers whose accounts we possess. Herodian describes how, during a fire in Rome, the entire possessions of some rich men were looted by criminals and the lower class, 'who mixed with the soldiers in order to do just this'.[22] After a fire in Nicomedia, its governor, Pliny the Younger, wrote that 'it is generally agreed that people stood watching the disaster without bothering themselves to do anything to stop it'; 'it would not have spread so far but for the apathy of the populace'.[23] In his eyes, this lack of interest showed how useless the population were and how in need of elite government. But perhaps, in the people's eyes, doing nothing was a perfectly reasonable response: they may have had little or nothing to lose, so why risk their lives defending it; or perhaps it was mainly the public buildings that were affected, which they could expect the elite to replace at their own cost in any case. Regrettably, their version of events does not survive. As Pliny the Younger comments, when apologising for giving details of crowd behaviour during the eruption of Vesuvius, 'of course these details are not important enough for history', and indeed seemed 'scarcely worth even putting in a letter'.[24]

Tacitus' account of the Great Fire in Rome of 64 CE gives us some sense of how ordinary people had different attitudes to risk. He describes how, when the fire first struck, rumours were rife, and the citizens ran about, asking 'where?', 'how did it happen?', 'what started it?' These were very different kinds of questions from those asked by later elite historians, who were concerned more about the damage to public property and what the event might be portending politically.[25] People wanted to know who or what was responsible, reflecting a desire for simple justice and accountability. They wanted to know exactly where it had spread, so that they could decide on their best course of action. What Tacitus condemned as mere rumour can be interpreted as a desperate attempt to gather information. Rumour served as a way for the people to publicise their own version of the crisis, which focused on their vulnerability. It challenged the kind of elite narrative, which was most concerned with the impact such an event might have on property and high politics.

Conclusion

The Roman world was full of what elite authors saw as the risks generated by the acquisition of empire. While all these writers approved of empire itself and saw Roman domination as a natural state of affairs, they refused to see wealth and social change as acceptable or inevitable by-products of

---

[22] Herodian 7.12.6–7.   [23] Pliny, *Letters* 10.33, after Loeb translation.
[24] Ibid. 6.20, Loeb translation.   [25] Dio Cassius 62.16–18.

imperial success. To them, these side effects all seemed to threaten the very social order that had generated the empire in the first place, and looked to their own forms of expertise to counteract these threats. Religious suppression, moralising and sumptuary legislation all aimed at preventing such changes from making further inroads into Roman society, and sought to return to an idealised past. Whether the Roman elite ever imagined that these measures could work in reality is hard to say. The authorities lacked the resources to enforce this legislative regime in any other than an exemplary way. Instead, we can see the hostility in elite sources, both legal and literary, as reflecting elite unease about the alternative behaviours operating so freely around them.

Moral and social risks acted as a powerful tool for the elite to articulate their view of what constituted the socially normal and normative. By dwelling on the novel and the unacceptable, they could generate a strong sense of how society should be run. For the emperor, as *pater patriae*, 'father of the nation', it became his duty to correct the errant behaviour of his household members, whatever their status in society. The metaphor of the emperor as father helped to spell out the form that social obedience should take, and also justified the threat and use of corrective punishment. The image therefore served to display imperial power, enforce domination and construct community. It articulated the aspirations of the regime: to be at the head of a well-ordered, interconnected and contented society. But above all, it advertised and asserted the new form of government's moral right to rule and legislate against what it saw as unacceptable risks.

Moral hazards were partly brought in as an explanation for past disaster, but partly also as a forward-looking action to prevent calamity from happening again. Fears for the future were expressed in backward-looking terms, based on traditional moral notions. This represented a moral construction of the world, whether past, present or future. Risk, for us, is a forward-looking concept, even if the reforms it generates are based on the analysis of previous events. The Romans also saw tradition as a reservoir of valuable resources that could be accessed but did so in order to create a future that was fashioned in the image of the past.

CHAPTER 6

Conclusion

Each society creates its own ways of coping with the uncertainties of the future. We have seen that the Romans used their own cultural forms to establish an intellectual relationship with the dangers that they faced. These means of dealing with risk displayed a strong element of traditional practice, intuition and collective experience. But a lack of understanding about the principles of probability did not mean they had no ability to conceptualise or, in part, manage those risks. Areas such as the law and finance show that the Romans also developed more conceptually sophisticated ways of understanding and controlling future uncertainty. Again, this was not based on mathematical calculation but on verbal reasoning and an informal, instinctive understanding of what was both likely to happen and what was a reasonable response to those outcomes. Modernity's interest in risk represents an intensification of previous practice rather than a sudden and complete innovation.[1]

What has occurred in modernity is a rise in a risk discourse and a change in the forms it takes. Partly this has been reflected in the application of the term to such a wide variety of areas: both objective and subjective dangers, as a measure of exposure to such dangers, the likelihood of such dangers arising and potential loss if they do. This may simply reflect a modern preference for a term that sounds exact, neutral and scientific.[2] But, as Beck has rightly noted, it also reflects a search for safety and security in a world where a feeling of insecurity has been increased by the very technologies that were designed to reduce it. 'Risk' now expresses all manner of anxieties relating to our control over what affects our bodies, our relationship to others, our livelihoods and the degree to which we are in control of

---

[1] See Beck and Kewell, *Risk*; also L. Krüger (ed.), *The Probabilistic Revolution*, 2 vols, Cambridge, MA: MIT Press, 1987, on statistical developments from 1800 to the 1950s.
[2] N. N. Taleb, *The Black Swan: The Impact of the Highly Improbable*, London: Allen Lane, 2007.

our own lives.³ In that sense, modern risk discourse reflects a way of constructing the future as a place where misfortune is no longer perceived as being the result of accident or divine will, but as the result of human failure to take into account the lessons of accurate calculation. From this kind of technical perspective, risk represents an objective phenomenon that needs only to be measured, predicted and then controlled.

But as the Roman case has also shown, assessing risk is never neutral. As Douglas has argued, risk and blame are inseparable, and when risks appear they generate a blame game against the supposed source of the contamination. In the modern world, risk has become part of a new form of moralising about what kinds of risk are acceptable and what should be done about those at-risk individuals who choose not to behave in an appropriate risk-averse and prudent manner.⁴ Risk discourse promotes what it sees as responsible behaviour, placing an expectation on individuals to be aware of how their own behaviour affects the degree of risk they are exposed to, but also seeks to mobilise a communal response against those who refuse to act in this way. Attitudes to risk, whether risk-loving or risk-averse, have therefore become a key way in which individuals construct their identity.

A Foucauldian response to this is to see modern risk discourse as being used by governmental systems to aid their control over the population.⁵ Risk is harnessed in this process to exaggerate anxieties and justify action against deviant behaviour, representing a new mode of surveillance and governmental control. It is the those in authority, advised by their own team of experts, who identify which individuals are most at risk (it is hard not to think of governmental responses during the Coronavirus pandemic in this regard). Again, the example of Roman sumptuary legislation has shown that there is nothing new in a government seeing certain activities as posing a threat and taking action to suppress them, albeit with a lesser degree of intensity. Beck's description of a risk society, where the old certainties have been lost, knowledge is contested and risk is perceived as widespread, does not seem so far from the situation in ancient Rome. However, there are undoubtedly differences. In particular, the modern

---

³ See the introduction to R. Muchembled, *Popular Culture and Elite Culture in France, 1400–1750*, trans. L. Cochrane, Baton Rouge: Louisiana State University Press, 1985.
⁴ Doyle and Ericson, *Risk and Morality*.
⁵ See G. Burchell, C. Gordon and P. Miller (eds), *The Foucault Effect: Studies in Governmentality*, Chicago: University of Chicago Press, 1991, esp. R. Castel, 'From dangerousness to risk', pp. 281–98. See also P. O'Malley, 'The uncertain promise of risk', *Australian and New Zealand Journal of Criminology*, 37 (2004), 323–42.

focus on the individual in risk discourse reflects a capitalist society's move away from the central place of community in the ancient world. But if we accept Beck's argument that modernity questions the outcomes of technological advances in terms of its production of risk, then it is possible to see a parallel process occurring in Rome, whereby Rome developed a heightened awareness of the risks that its own military success had created.

Shaw has argued that the Romans had a fragmented and short-term understanding of the future.[6] This means that when we look at the Roman evidence, we find little that suggests any large-scale forward planning, specifically 'anything that might count as strategic thinking about the state's position *vis-à-vis* its future resources'. Military manuals, for example, give various solutions to specific problems but they represent tactics rather than long-term military planning. Overall, Shaw argues, Roman understanding of the future lay somewhere between the endless repetition of the present as experienced by a traditional peasant and a modern, complex and fully envisaged future. Using an analogy of painting, he argues that the Roman concept of the future seems to have been located 'somewhere between the "eternal present" . . . and the creation of "modern perspective" in the fourteenth and fifteenth centuries in Western Europe'. This was not owing to a lack of techniques, since these were available to them. Instead, the Romans chose not to do so, and 'systematically subordinated the possible use of single-point perspective to other more important aims'. By contrast, the modern world sees the world in terms of a grid of single-point visual perspective. This development was paralleled, in a non-accidental way, in other spheres of human activity, which saw the emergence of banks, government debt markets, double-entry bookkeeping and mathematical calculations of future risk assessment. The modern approach is distinguished by three characteristics: seeing the future as a reservoir of valuable resources that could be tapped in the present; that the concept is widely accepted and understood, rather than just being an elite idea; and that present-day activity is oriented to planning and developing the future as it is imagined it should be.

How does this compare with Roman approaches to understanding and dealing with risk? There are clearly some similarities:

1. As I have argued, the development of ideas concerning risk is best seen as a continuum and that, as with ideas about the future, Roman

---

[6] Shaw, 'Did the Romans have a future?'.

concepts sit somewhere between basic and more advanced modern notions.
2. Most Roman ways of dealing with uncertainty and future danger are concerned with practical issues of the moment or near-term future. Even where the issue is a long-term one, such as life expectancy in Ulpian's Table, the thinking is designed to solve an immediate tax problem not to compute an accurate assessment of mortality.
3. More systematic attempts to control risk, especially those found in the law, still try to establish principles for the purpose of practical application.
4. Even then, it is hard to draw parallels between different areas of systematic thinking. As with the future, thinking about risk was more fragmented and did not seek to apply principles learned in one area to other cognate fields.
5. Most of the more sophisticated thinking about risk comes from a small section of society. Although we can discern various elements of more popular attitudes to risk, these are articulated in less intellectual ways and the quantity of evidence for them is modest in comparison.

There are some areas where Roman action relating to risk could be seen as delivering a longer-term vision:

1. Military planning did include the maintenance of a standing army as well as the construction of military infrastructure, such as an extensive road network, fortified legionary bases and grain stores, reflecting an awareness that Rome's enemies would continue to exist far into the future.
2. Building in the urban context sometimes tried to make improvements to planning based on an improved understanding of certain risks, most notably perhaps in Nero's ruling that, after the Great Fire of 64 CE, Rome should be rebuilt in stone, with wider streets and lower-rise buildings.

That said, it is clear that such longer-term risk control was not the norm and, in the case of Nero, possibly reflected a knee-jerk response to a self-created crisis rather than a thoughtful piece of town planning. It can also be said that long-term military infrastructure was understood as a permanent, never-ending requirement and so represented not so much a vision of a risk-reduced future but an eternal necessity of the ancient state.

As with the future, Roman ideas about risk displayed a mixture of both basic and relatively sophisticated understanding. The areas where the greatest development can be found – in the military, financial and legal spheres – reflect a militaristic, legalistic and strongly hierarchical society where what mattered most was keeping control of great areas of territory, maintaining the social order that controlled the population and upholding the property rights of the few. There was no perceived need to develop the notion of risk outside of these areas. Perhaps the greatest difference is the attitude towards time. Whereas the modern understanding of risk sees it as a concept concerned with changing the future for the better, the Romans saw risk as something that might cause them to deviate from the tried-and-tested methods and morals of the past.

Further Reading

A good introduction to the concept of risk can be found in D. Lupton, *Risk*, 2nd edition, Abingdon: Routledge, 2013. Discussion concerning the definition of risk is available in A. Burgess, A., Alemanno and J. Zinn (eds), *Routledge Handbook of Risk Studies*, London: Routledge, 2016, as well as N. Luhmann, *Risk: A Sociological Theory*, trans. R. Barrett, New York: de Gruyter, 1993, pp. 1–31, 'The concept of risk'. Also of use are O. Renn, 'Concepts of risk: a classification', in S. Krimsky and D. Golding (eds), *Social Theories of Risk*, Westport, CT: Praeger, 1992, pp. 53–79, and J. O. Zinn (ed.), *Social Theories of Risk and Uncertainty: An Introduction*, Oxford: Blackwell, 2008.

On the concept of risk in relation to finance in the modern world, see P. Faulkner, A. Feduzi and J. Runde, 'Unknowns, Black Swans and the risk/uncertainty distinction', *Cambridge Journal of Economics*, 41 (2017), 1279–302, and A. Doyle and D. Ericson, *Uncertain Business: Risk, Insurance, and the Limits of Knowledge*, Toronto: Toronto University Press, 2004.

On the history and development of the term 'risk' as a concept, the best overviews are provided by M. Beck and B. Kewell, *Risk: A Study of Its Origins, History and Politics*, New Jersey: World Scientific, 2014 and I. Hacking, *The Emergence of Probability: A Philosophical Study of Early Ideas about Probability, Induction and Statistical Inference*, 2nd edition, Cambridge: Cambridge University Press, 2006. Hacking's book, *The Taming of Chance*, Cambridge: Cambridge University Press, 1990 is also useful. P. L. Bernstein, *Against the Gods: The Remarkable Story of Risk*, New York: John Wiley, 1996, is interesting, although it has little to say about the pre-modern world.

The influential idea of a 'Risk Society' is to be found in U. Beck, *Risikogesellschaft: Auf dem Weg in eine andere Moderne*, Frankfurt: Suhrkamp, 1986, translated as *Risk Society: Towards a New Modernity*, trans. M. Ritter, London: Sage, 1992. Other sociological approaches to risk as a modern phenomenon can be seen in J. Franklin (ed.), *The Politics of Risk Society*, Maldon, MA: Polity, 1998.

Mary Douglas has written a number of important works on risk from an anthropological perspective, including 'Risk as a forensic resource: from "chance" to "danger"', *Daedalus*, 119 (1990), 1–16, *Risk and Blame: Essays in Cultural Theory*, London: Routledge, 1992, and, in collaboration with A. Wildavsky, *Risk and Culture: An Essay on the Selection of Technical and Environmental Dangers*, Berkeley: University of California Press, 1982. Other fruitful anthropological approaches to risk can be found in P. Halstead and J. O'Shea, *Bad Year Economics: Cultural Responses to Risk and Uncertainty*, Cambridge: Cambridge University Press, 1989, and G. Burchell, C. Gordon and P. Miller (eds), *The Foucault Effect: Studies in Governmentality*, Chicago: University of Chicago Press, 1991, especially the chapter by R. Castel, 'From dangerousness to risk', pp. 281–98.

On the relationship between gender and vulnerability to risk, see E. Enarson and P. G. Dhar Chakrabarti, *Women, Gender and Disaster: Global Issues and Initiatives*, London: Sage, 2009, and H. Rodríguez, E. L. Quarantelli and R. R. Dynes (eds), *Handbook of Disaster Research*, New York: Springer, 2007, ch. 8, 'Gender and disaster: foundations and directions', pp. 130–46. On risk in daily life, see J. Tulloch and D. Lupton, *Risk and Everyday Life*, London: Sage, 2003, and I. Wilkinson, *Risk, Vulnerability and Everyday Life*, London: Routledge, 2008. On the growth of risk-taking as a positive choice, see S. Lyng (ed.), *Edgework: The Sociology of Risk Taking*, London: Routledge, 2005.

On pre-modern ways of dealing with uncertainty, the most useful are the works by J. Franklin, *The Science of Conjecture: Evidence and Probability before Pascal*, Baltimore, MD: Johns Hopkins University Press, 2001, and R. Brown, 'History versus Hacking on probability', *History of European Ideas*, 8 (1987), 655–73.

On risk in the ancient world, see Cam Grey's two pieces, *Constructing Communities in the Late Roman Countryside*, Cambridge: Cambridge University Press, 2011, and 'Risk and vulnerability on the Campanian plain: the Vesuvius eruption of A.D. 472', *Journal of Interdisciplinary History*, 51 (2020), 1–37, the latter analysing how social structures and environmental factors combined to create vulnerabilities in relation to the eruption of Vesuvius. Mary Beard has considered the positive value placed on risk in the Roman world in her 'Risk and the humanities: alea iacta est', in L. Skinns, M. Scott and T. Cox (eds), *Risk*, Cambridge: Cambridge University Press, 2011, pp. 85–108. For risk and risk-control strategies adopted in a non-elite context, see J. Toner, *Popular Culture in Ancient Rome*, Cambridge: Polity, 2009, pp. 11–53.

Discussion of ancient ideas concerning chance and uncertainty can be found in S. Sambursky, 'On the possible and probable in Ancient Greece', *Osiris*, 12 (1956), 35–48, and, more profitably, in E. Eidinow, *Luck, Fate, and Fortune*, Oxford: Oxford University Press, 2011. The work by Ulrike Ehmig addresses many specific aspects of ancient perceptions of risk, such as her 'Subjektive und faktische Risiken: Votivgründe und Todesursachen in lateinischen Inschriften als Beispiele für Nachrichtenauswahl in der römischen Kaiserzeit', *Chiron*, 43 (2013), 127–98, which compares the causes of death on tombstones with the causes of anxiety recorded in votive inscriptions to see if perceptions of risk may have affected how the real level of underlying risk was seen.

Ancient ideas of the future are discussed in J. J. Price and K. Berthelot (eds), *The Future of Rome: Roman, Greek, Jewish and Christian Visions*, Cambridge:

Cambridge University Press, 2020, and for Rome, B. D. Shaw, 'Did the Romans have a future?', *Journal of Roman Studies*, 109 (2019), 1–26. On the use of divination to manage uncertainty in the ancient Greek world, see K. Beerden, *Worlds Full of Signs: Ancient Greek Divination in Context*, Leiden: Brill, 2013 and E. Eidinow, *Oracles, Curses, and Risk among the Ancient Greeks*, Oxford: Oxford University Press, 2007, and on the use of magic, J. G. Gager (ed.), *Curse Tablets and Binding Spells from the Ancient World*, Oxford: Oxford University Press, 1992.

The risks posed by low life-expectancy are revealed in discussions of the demography of the Roman world, see T. G. Parkin, *Demography and Roman Society*, Baltimore, MD: Johns Hopkins University Press, 1992, and W. Scheidel, *Death on the Nile: Disease and the Demography of Roman Egypt*, Mnemosyne Supplements, Leiden and Boston: Brill, 2001.

Works that deal with the risks posed by disasters in Antiquity, include J. Toner, *Roman Disasters*, Cambridge: Polity, 2013 and J. J. Walsh, *The Great Fire of Rome: Life and Death in the Ancient City*, Baltimore, MD: Johns Hopkins University Press, 2019. Scheidel and Harper have both provided comparative historical studies of plagues and pandemics and, in Scheidel's case, war: see W. Scheidel, *The Great Leveler: Violence and the History of Inequality from the Stone Age to the Twenty-First Century*, Princeton, NJ: Princeton University Press, 2017, and K. Harper, *Plagues upon the Earth: Disease and the Course of Human History*, Princeton, NJ: Princeton University Press, 2021. On the Justinianic plague, see also L. K. Little (ed.), *Plague and the End of Antiquity: The Pandemic of 541–750*, Cambridge: Cambridge University Press, 2007. Debate about the risks posed by climatic conditions and changes in late Antiquity can be found in P. Sarris, 'Climate and disease', in E. Hermans (ed.), *A Companion to the Global Early Middle Ages*, Leeds: Arc Humanities Press, 2020, pp. 511–38. Kyle Harper discusses the impact of both plague and climate change in *The Fate of Rome: Climate, Disease, and the End of an Empire*, Princeton, NJ: Princeton University Press, 2017. On the seriousness of the impact of the Justinianic plague, see L. Mordechai and M. Eisenberg, 'Rejecting catastrophe: the case of the Justinianic plague', *Past & Present*, 244 (2019), 3–50, and, in response, P. Sarris, 'New approaches to the plague of Justinian', *Past and Present*, 254 (2022), 315–46.

Useful studies of the risk of flood and natural disaster in the Roman world are to be found in G. S. Aldrete, *Floods of the Tiber in Ancient Rome*, Baltimore, MD: Johns Hopkins University Press, 2007, and M. Ronin, 'The perception of natural risks of earthquakes and floods in the Roman world', *Historia*, 71 (2022), 362–89. For studies of risk in relation to ancient peasant culture, see P. Garnsey, *Famine and Food Supply in the Graeco-Roman World: Responses to Risk and Crisis*, Cambridge: Cambridge University Press, 1988, and T. W. Gallant, *Risk and Survival in Ancient Greece: Reconstructing the Rural Domestic Economy*, Cambridge: Polity, 1991. On Roman peasant culture, see Bowes, K. (ed.), *The Roman Peasant Project 2009–2014: Excavating the Roman Rural Poor*, University Museum monograph, 154, Philadelphia: University of Pennsylvania Museum of Archaeology and Anthropology, 2020.

An overview of the Roman financial system can be obtained in J. Andreau, *Banking and Business in the Roman World*, Cambridge: Cambridge University Press, 1999. The Roman enjoyment of risk-taking in the form of gambling can be explored in J. Toner, *Leisure and Ancient Rome*, Cambridge: Polity, 1995, pp. 89–101, and 'The intellectual life of the Roman non-elite', in L. Grig (ed.), *Popular Culture in the Ancient World*, Cambridge: Cambridge University Press, 2016, pp. 167–88, as well as N. Purcell, 'Literate games: Roman urban society and the game of alea', *Past & Present*, 147 (1995), 3–37.

Bibliography

Aldrete, G. S., *Floods of the Tiber in Ancient Rome*, Baltimore, MD: Johns Hopkins University Press, 2007.
Alexander, J. C., and Smith, P., 'Social science and salvation: risk society as a mythic discourse', *Zeitschrift für Soziologie*, 25 (1996), 251–62.
Anderson, H. E. III, 'Risk, shipping, and Roman law', *Tulane Maritime Law Journal*, 34 (2009), 183–210.
Andreau, J., *Banking and Business in the Roman World*, Cambridge: Cambridge University Press, 1999.
Beard, M., 'Risk and the humanities: alea iacta est', in L. Skinns, M. Scott and T. Cox (eds), *Risk*, Cambridge: Cambridge University Press, 2011, pp. 85–108.
Beck, M., and Kewell, B., *Risk: A Study of Its Origins, History and Politics*, New Jersey: World Scientific, 2014.
Beck, U., 'From industrial society to the Risk Society: questions of survival, social structure and ecological enlightenment', *Theory, Culture and Society*, 9 (1992), 97–123.
 Risikogesellschaft: Auf dem Weg in eine andere Moderne, Frankfurt: Suhrkamp, 1986, translated as *Risk Society: Towards a New Modernity*, trans. M. Ritter, London: Sage, 1992.
Beerden, K., *Worlds Full of Signs: Ancient Greek Divination in Context*, Leiden: Brill, 2013.
Bennett, S. (ed.), *Innovative Thinking in Risk, Crisis and Disaster Management*, Farnham: Gower, 2012.
Bernstein, P. L., *Against the Gods: The Remarkable Story of Risk*, New York: John Wiley, 1996.
Betz, H. D. (ed.), *The Greek Magical Papyri in Translation, Including the Demotic Spells*, Chicago: University of Chicago Press, 1992.
Billeter, G., *Geschichte des Zinsfusses im griechisch-römischen Altertum bis auf Justinian*, Leipzig: Teubner, 1898.
Blastland, M., and Spiegelhalter, D., *The Norm Chronicles: Stories and Numbers about Danger*, London: Profile, 2013.
Boholm, A., 'Comparative studies of risk perception: a review of twenty years of research', *Journal of Risk Research*, 1 (1998), 135–63.

Bowes, K. (ed.), *The Roman Peasant Project 2009–2014: Excavating the Roman Rural Poor*, University museum monograph, 154, Philadelphia: University of Pennsylvania Museum of Archaeology and Anthropology, 2020.

Boyne, R., *Risk*, London: Open University Press, 2003.

Bradley, K. R., *Discovering the Roman Family: Studies in Roman Social History*, Oxford: Oxford University Press, 1991.

Breakwell, G. M., *The Psychology of Risk*, Cambridge: Cambridge University Press, 2007.

Brown, P., *Poverty and Leadership in the Later Roman Empire*, London and Hanover, NH: University Press of New England, 2002.

Brown, R., 'History versus Hacking on probability', *History of European Ideas*, 8 (1987), 655–73.

Burchell, G., Gordon, C. and Miller, P. (eds), *The Foucault Effect: Studies in Governmentality*, Chicago: University of Chicago Press, 1991.

Burgess, A., Alemanno, A. and Zinn, J. (eds), *Routledge Handbook of Risk Studies*, London: Routledge, 2016.

Candy, P., and Mataix Ferrándiz, E. (eds), *Roman Law and Maritime Commerce*, Edinburgh: Edinburgh University Press, 2022.

Carrithers, M., *Why Humans Have Cultures: Explaining Anthropology and Social Diversity*, Oxford: Oxford University Press, 1992.

Casson, L., *Travel in the Ancient World*, London: Allen & Unwin, 1974.

Castel, R., 'From dangerousness to risk', in G. Burchell, C. Gordon and P. Miller (eds), *The Foucault Effect: Studies in Governmentality*, Chicago: University of Chicago Press, 1991, pp. 281–98.

Cheyette, F. L., 'The disappearance of the ancient landscape and the climate anomaly of the early Middle Ages: a question to be pursued', *Early Medieval Europe*, 16 (2008), 127–65.

The Chronicle of Pseudo-Joshua the Stylite, trans. F. R. Trombley and J. W. Watt, Liverpool: Liverpool University Press, 2000.

The Chronicle of Zuqnīn, parts III and IV: AD 488–775, trans. A. Harrak, Toronto: Pontifical Institute of Mediaeval Studies, 1999.

Ciecka, J. E., 'Ulpian's Table and the value of life annuities and usufructs', *Journal of Legal Economics*, 19 (2012), 7–15.

Closs, V. M., *While Rome Burned: Fire, Leadership, and Urban Disaster in the Roman Cultural Imagination*, Ann Arbor: University of Michigan Press, 2020.

Daly, L. W. (ed.), *Aesop without Morals: The Famous Fables, and a Life of Aesop*, New York: T. Yoseloff, 1961.

David, F. N., 'Dicing and gaming (a note on the history of probability)', *Biometrika*, 42 (1955), 1–15.

  Games, Gods and Gambling: The Origins and History of Probability and Statistical Ideas from the Earliest Times to the Newtonian Era, London: C. Griffin, 1962.

De Romanis, F., *The Indo-Roman Pepper Trade and the Muziris Papyrus*, Oxford: Oxford University Press, 2020.

De Ste. Croix, G. E. M., 'Ancient Greek and Roman maritime loans', in H. C. Edey and B. S. Yamey (eds), *Debits, Credits, Finance and Profits*, London: Sweet and Maxwell, 1974, pp. 41–59.

De Vries, T., and Zwalve, W. J., 'Roman actuarial science and Ulpian's life expectancy table', in L. de Ligt, E. A. Hemelrijk and H. W. Singor (eds), *Roman Rule and Civic Life: Local and Regional Perspectives*, Leiden: Brill, 2004, pp. 275–97.

Dean, M., 'Risk, calculable and incalculable', *Soziale Welt – Zeitschrift für Sozialwissenschaftliche Forschung und Praxis*, 49 (1998), 25–42.

Deeg, P., *Der Kaiser und die Katastrophe: Untersuchungen zum politischen Umgang mit Umweltkatastrophen im Prinzipat (31 v. Chr. bis 192 n. Chr.)*, Stuttgart: Franz Steiner, 2019.

Denney, D., *Risk and Society*, London: Sage, 2005.

Dorigo, W., *Late Roman Painting: A Study of Pictorial Records, 30 BC–AD 500*, trans. J. Cleugh and J. Warrington, London: Dent, 1971.

Dörner, D., *The Logic of Failure: Recognizing and Avoiding Error in Complex Situations*, trans. R. and R. Kimber, Reading, MA: Addison-Wesley, 1996.

Douglas, M., 'Risk as a forensic resource: from "chance" to "danger"', *Daedalus*, 119 (1990), 1–16.

Risk and Blame: Essays in Cultural Theory, London: Routledge, 1992.

Douglas, M., and Wildavsky, A., *Risk and Culture: An Essay on the Selection of Technical and Environmental Dangers*, Berkeley: University of California Press, 1982.

Doyle, A., and Ericson, D., *Uncertain Business: Risk, Insurance, and the Limits of Knowledge*, Toronto: Toronto University Press, 2004.

Doyle, A., and Ericson, D. (eds), *Risk and Morality*, Toronto: University of Toronto Press, 2003.

Du Plessis, P. J., *Letting and Hiring in Roman Legal Thought 27BCE–284CE*, Leiden: Brill, 2012.

Du Plessis, P. J., Ando, C. and Tuori, K. (eds), *The Oxford Handbook of Roman Law and Society*, Oxford: Oxford University Press, 2016.

Duncan-Jones, R., *Money and Government in the Roman Empire*, Cambridge: Cambridge University Press, 1994.

Ehmig, U., 'Antiker Umgang mit Wahrscheinlichem: einige Beobachtungen in den dokumentarischen Quellen', *Eirene*, 49 (2013), 90–116.

'Subjektive und faktische Risiken.Votivgründe und Todesursachen in lateinischen Inschriften als Beispiele für Nachrichtenauswahl in der römischen Kaiserzeit', *Chiron*, 43 (2013), 127–98.

Eidinow, E., *Luck, Fate, and Fortune*, Oxford: Oxford University Press, 2011.

Oracles, Curses, and Risk among the Ancient Greeks, Oxford: Oxford University Press, 2007.

Elsner, J., and Masters, J. (eds), *Reflections of Nero: Culture, History, and Representation*, London: Duckworth, 1994.

Enarson, E., and Dhar Chakrabarti, P. G., *Women, Gender and Disaster: Global Issues and Initiatives*, London: Sage, 2009.

Erdkamp, P., *Hunger and the Sword: Warfare and Food Supply in Roman Republican Wars (264–30 B.C.)*, Amsterdam: J. C. Gieben, 1998.
  (ed.), *A Companion to the Roman Army*, Oxford: Blackwell, 2007.
Faulkner, P., Feduzi, A. and Runde, J., 'Unknowns, Black Swans and the risk/uncertainty distinction', *Cambridge Journal of Economics*, 41 (2017), 1279–1302.
Foster, G. M., 'Peasant society and the image of limited good', *American Anthropologist*, 67 (1965), 293–315.
Fothergill, A., 'Gender, risk, and disaster', *International Journal of Mass Emergencies and Disasters*, 14 (1996), 33–56.
Franklin, J., *The Science of Conjecture: Evidence and Probability before Pascal*, Baltimore, MD: Johns Hopkins University Press, 2001.
  (ed.), *The Politics of Risk Society*, Maldon, MA: Polity, 1998.
Freedgood, E., *Victorian Writing about Risk: Imagining a Safe England in a Dangerous World*, Cambridge: Cambridge University Press, 2000.
Frier, B. W., 'Demography', in A. K. Bowman, P. Garnsey and D. Rathbone (eds), *The Cambridge Ancient History XI: The High Empire, A.D. 70–192*, 2nd edition, Cambridge: Cambridge University Press, 2000, pp. 787–816.
  'Roman life expectancy: Ulpian's evidence', *Harvard Studies in Classical Philology*, 86 (1982), 213–51.
Gager, J. G. (ed.), *Curse Tablets and Binding Spells from the Ancient World*, Oxford: Oxford University Press, 1992.
Gallant, T. W., *Risk and Survival in Ancient Greece: Reconstructing the Rural Domestic Economy*, Cambridge: Polity, 1991.
Garland, D., 'The rise of risk', in A. Doyle and D. Ericson (eds), *Risk and Morality*, Toronto: University of Toronto Press, 2003, pp. 48–86.
Garnsey, P., *Famine and Food Supply in the Graeco-Roman World: Responses to Risk and Crisis*, Cambridge: Cambridge University Press, 1988.
Geertz, C., *The Interpretation of Cultures: Selected Essays*, New York: Basic Books, 1973.
Giddens, A., *Modernity and Self-identity: Self and Society in the Late Modern Age*, Cambridge: Polity, 1991.
  Runaway World: How Globalisation Is Reshaping Our Lives, London: Profile, 1999.
Graf, F., 'Rolling the dice for an answer', in S. I. Johnston and P. T. Struck (eds), *Mantikê: Studies in Ancient Divination*, Leiden: Brill, 2005, pp. 51–97.
Green, C. M. C., *Roman Religion and the Cult of Diana at Aricia*, Cambridge: Cambridge University Press, 2007.
Green, M. H., 'When Numbers Don't Count: Changing Perspectives on the Justinianic plague', *Eidolon*, 18 (2019). https://eidolon.pub/when-numbers-dont-count-56a2b3c3d07.
Greenwood, M., 'A statistical Mare's Nest?', *Journal of the Royal Statistical Society*, 103 (1940), 246–8.
Grey, C., *Constructing Communities in the Late Roman Countryside*, Cambridge: Cambridge University Press, 2011.

'Risk and vulnerability on the Campanian plain: the Vesuvius eruption of A.D. 472', *Journal of Interdisciplinary History*, 51 (2020), 1–37.

Haberman, S., and Sibbett, T. A. (eds), *History of Actuarial Science*, vol. 1, London: William Pickering, 1995.

Hacking, I., *The Emergence of Probability: A Philosophical Study of Early Ideas about Probability, Induction and Statistical Inference*, 2nd edition, Cambridge: Cambridge University Press, 2006.

'Risk and dirt', in A. Doyle and D. Ericson (eds), *Risk and Morality*, Toronto: University of Toronto Press, 2003, pp. 22–47.

The Taming of Chance, Cambridge: Cambridge University Press, 1990.

Hald, A., *A History of Probability and Statistics and Their Applications before 1750*, Hoboken, NJ: John Wiley, 2003.

Haldon, J., et al., 'Plagues, climate change, and the end of an empire: a response to Kyle Harper's *The Fate of Rome* (1): Climate', *History Compass*, 16 (2018). https://compass.onlinelibrary.wiley.com/doi/abs/10.1111/hic3.12508.

'Plagues, climate change, and the end of an empire: a response to Kyle Harper's *The Fate of Rome* (2): plagues and a crisis of empire', *History Compass*, 16 (2018). https://compass.onlinelibrary.wiley.com/doi/full/10.1111/hic3.12506.

'Plagues, climate change, and the end of an empire: a response to Kyle Harper's *The Fate of Rome* (3): disease, agency and collapse', *History Compass*, 16 (2018). https://compass.onlinelibrary.wiley.com/doi/full/10.1111/hic3.12507.

Halstead, P., and O'Shea, J., *Bad Year Economics: Cultural Responses to Risk and Uncertainty*, Cambridge: Cambridge University Press, 1989.

Hammond, M. *(trans)* and Thonemann, P. (introduction), *Artemidorus: The Interpretation of Dreams*, Oxford: Oxford University Press, 2020.

Hansen, W. (ed.), *Anthology of Ancient Greek Popular Literature*, Bloomington: Indiana University Press, 1998.

Hansson, S. O., *The Ethics of Risk: Ethical Analysis in an Uncertain World*, Basingstoke: Palgrave Macmillan, 2013.

Harper, K., *The Fate of Rome: Climate, Disease, and the End of an Empire*, Princeton, NJ: Princeton University Press, 2017.

'Integrating the natural sciences and Roman History: challenges and prospects', *History Compass*, 16 (2018). https://doi.org/10.1111/hic3.12520.

Plagues upon the Earth: Disease and the Course of Human History, Princeton, NJ: Princeton University Press, 2021.

Homer, S., and Sylla, R., *A History of Interest Rates*, 3rd edition, New Brunswick: Rutgers University Press, 1991.

Hopkins, K., *Conquerors and Slaves*, Cambridge: Cambridge University Press, 1978.

Hopkins, K, 'On the probable age structure of the Roman population', *Population Studies*, 20 (1966), 245–64.

Horden, P., and Purcell, N., *The Corrupting Sea: A Study of Mediterranean History*, Oxford: Blackwell, 2000.

Horsfall, N., *The Culture of the Roman Plebs*, London: Duckworth, 2003.

Horsley, G. H. R., and Mitchell, S. (eds), *The Inscriptions of Central Pisidia*, Bonn: Habelt, 2000.
Jakab, É., 'Risikomanagement bei den Naukleroi', in N. Benke and F.-S. Meissel (eds), *Antike – Recht – Geschichte*, Frankfurt: P. Lang, 2009, pp. 73–88.
  Risikomanagement beim Weinkauf: Periculum und Praxis im Imperium Romanum, Munich: C. H. Beck, 2009.
Joffe, H., *Risk and 'the Other'*, Cambridge: Cambridge University Press, 1999.
Johns, L. S. et al., *The Effects of Nuclear War*, Washington, DC: Library of Congress, 1979.
Johnston, D., *Roman Law in Context*, Cambridge: Cambridge University Press, 1999.
  The Roman Law of Trusts, Oxford: Clarendon, 1988.
  (ed.), *The Cambridge Companion to Roman Law*, Cambridge: Cambridge University Press, 2015.
Klingshirn, W., 'Christian divination in late Roman Gaul: the *Sortes Sangallenses*', in S. I. Johnston and P. T. Struck (eds), *Mantikê: Studies in Ancient Divination*, Leiden: Brill, 2005, pp. 99–128.
Knight, F. H., *Risk, Uncertainty and Profit*, Boston: Houghton Mifflin, 1921.
Krimsky, S., and Golding, D. (eds), *Social Theories of Risk*, Westport, CT: Praeger, 1992.
Krüger, L. (ed.), *The Probabilistic Revolution*, 2 vols, Cambridge, MA: MIT Press, 1987.
Laes, C., 'Children and accidents in Roman Antiquity', *Ancient Society*, 34 (2004), 153–70.
Le Bohec, Y. (ed.), *The Encylcopedia of the Roman Army*, 3 vols, Chichester: Wiley Blackwell, 2015.
Lehoux, D., *Astronomy, Weather, and Calendars in the Ancient World: Parapegmata and Related Texts in Classical and Near-Eastern societies*, Cambridge: Cambridge University Press, 2007.
Lendon, J. E., *Empire of Honour: The Art of Government in the Roman World*, Oxford: Clarendon, 1997.
Levinson, S. C., and Brown, P., *Politeness: Some Universals in Language Usage*, Cambridge: Cambridge University Press, 1987.
Little, L. K., 'Plague historians in lab coats', *Past and Present*, 213 (2011), 267–90.
  (ed.), *Plague and the End of Antiquity: The Pandemic of 541–750*, Cambridge: Cambridge University Press, 2007.
Living with Risk: The British Medical Association Guide, Chichester: Wiley, 1987.
Luhmann, N., *Risk: A Sociological Theory*, trans. R. Barrett, New York: de Gruyter, 1993.
Lupton, D., *Risk*, 2nd edition, Abingdon: Routledge, 2013.
  (ed.), *Risk and Socio-cultural Theory*, Cambridge: Cambridge University Press, 1999.
Lyng, S. (ed.), *Edgework: The Sociology of Risk Taking*, London: Routledge, 2005.
MacCormack, G., 'Dolus, culpa, custodia and diligentia – criteria of liability or content of obligation', *Index*, 22 (1996), 189–209.

'Further on periculum', *BIDR*, 1979 (1982), 11–40.
'Periculum', *Zeitschrift der Savigny-Stiftung für Rechtsgeschichte: Romanistische Abteilung*, 96 (1979), 129–72.
MacMullen, R., *Roman Social Relations, 50 B.C. to A.D. 284*, New Haven, CT: Yale University Press, 1974.
Macve, R. H., 'Some glosses on "Greek and Roman accounting"', *History of Political Thought*, 6 (1985), 233–64.
Markowitz, H. M., 'Portfolio selection', *Journal of Finance*, 7 (1952), 77–91.
McCambley, C., 'Against those who practice usury by Gregory of Nyssa', *Greek Orthodox Theological Review*, 36 (1991), 287–302.
McCormick, M., 'Climates of history, histories of climate: from history to archaeoscience', *Journal of Interdisciplinary History*, 50 (2019), 3–30.
Meier, M. 'The "Justinianic plague": an "inconsequential pandemic"? A reply', *Medizinhistorisches Journal*, 55 (2020), 172–99.
Millett, P., 'Maritime loans and the structure of credit in fourth-century Athens', in P. Garnsey, K. Hopkins and C. R. Whittaker (eds), *Trade in the Ancient Economy*, London: Chatto & Windus, 1983, pp. 36–52.
Mordechai, L., and Eisenberg, M., 'Rejecting catastrophe: the case of the Justinianic plague', *Past & Present*, 244 (2019), 3–50.
Morgan, T., *Popular Morality in the Early Roman Empire*, Cambridge: Cambridge University Press, 2007.
Morley, N., 'Decadence as a theory of history', *New Literary History*, 35 (2004), 573–85.
Trade in Classical Antiquity, Cambridge: Cambridge University Press, 2007.
Muchembled, R., *Popular Culture and Elite Culture in France, 1400–1750*, trans. L. Cochrane, Baton Rouge: Louisiana State University Press, 1985.
Nacol, E. C., *An Age of Risk: Politics and Economy in Early Modern Britain*, Princeton, NJ: Princeton University Press, 2016.
Newbold, R. F., 'The reporting of earthquakes, fires and floods by ancient historians', *Proceedings of the African Classical Association*, 16 (1982), 28–36.
O'Malley, P., *Crime and Risk*, Los Angeles: Sage, 2010.
Risk, Uncertainty and Government, London: GlassHouse, 2004.
'The uncertain promise of risk', *Australian and New Zealand Journal of Criminology*, 37 (2004), 323–42.
Obelkevich, J., 'Proverbs and social history', in P. Burke and R. Porter (eds), *The Social History of Language*, Cambridge: Cambridge University Press, 1987, pp. 43–72.
Oleson, J. P. (ed.), *The Oxford Handbook of Engineering and Technology in the Classical World*, Oxford: Oxford University Press, 2008.
Parkin, A. R., *Poverty in the Early Roman Empire: Ancient and Modern Conceptions and Constructs*, unpublished PhD dissertation, Cambridge University, 2001.
'"You do him no service": an exploration of pagan almsgiving', in M. Atkins and R. Osborne (eds), *Poverty in the Roman World*, Cambridge: Cambridge University Press, 2006, pp. 60–82.

Parkin, T. G., *Demography and Roman Society*, Baltimore, MD: Johns Hopkins University Press, 1992.
Pearson, E. S. and Kendall, M. G. (eds), *Studies in the History of Statistics and Probability*, 2 vols, London: C. Griffin, 1970.
Peddie, J., *The Roman War Machine*, Stroud: Alan Sutton,1994.
Pflaumer, P., 'Estimations of the Roman life expectancy using Ulpian's Table', *JSM Proceedings, Social Statistics Section*, Alexandria, VA: American Statistical Association, 2666–80. http://dx.doi.org/10.17877/DE290R-16456.
Poitras, G., *The Early History of Financial Economics, 1478–1776*, Cheltenham: Edward Elgar, 2000.
Price, J. J., and Berthelot, K. (eds), *The Future of Rome: Roman, Greek, Jewish and Christian Visions*, Cambridge: Cambridge University Press, 2020.
Price, S. R., 'The future of dreams: from Freud to Artemidorus', *Past & Present*, 113 (1986), 3–37.
Purcell, N., 'Literate games: Roman urban society and the game of alea', *Past & Present*, 147 (1995), 3–37.
Rathbone, D. W., 'The financing of maritime commerce in the Roman empire, (I–II AD)', in E. Lo Cascio (ed.), *Credito e moneta nel mondo romano*, Bari, Italy: Edipuglia, 2003, pp. 197–229.
Renn, O., 'Concepts of risk: a classification', in S. Krimsky and D. Golding (eds), *Social Theories of Risk*, Westport, CT: Praeger, 1992, pp. 53–79.
Rigakos, G., and Law, A., 'Risk, realism and the politics of resistance', *Critical Sociology*, 35 (2009), 79–103.
Riggsby, A. M., *Roman Law and the Legal World of the Romans*, Cambridge: Cambridge University Press, 2010.
Rodríguez, H., Quarantelli, E. L. and Dynes, R. R. (eds), *Handbook of Disaster Research*, New York: Springer, 2007.
Ronin, M., 'The perception of natural risks of earthquakes and floods in the Roman world', *Historia*, 71 (2022), 362–89.
Rosa, E. A., 'Metatheoretical foundations for post-normal risk', *Journal of Risk Research*, 1 (1998), 15–44.
Roth, J. P., *The Logistics of the Roman Army at War (264 B.C.–A.D. 235)*, Leiden: Brill, 1999.
Rougé, J., 'Prêt et société maritimes dans le monde romain', in J. H. D'Arms and E. C. Kopff (eds), *The Seaborne Commerce of Ancient Rome*, Rome: American Academy in Rome, 1980, pp. 291–303.
Rüpke, R., *Religion of the Romans*, trans. R. Gordon, Cambridge: Polity, 2007.
Sabin P. et al. (eds), *The Cambridge History of Greek and Roman Warfare*, 2 vols, Cambridge: Cambridge University Press, 2007.
Sallares, R., *The Ecology of the Ancient Greek World*, London: Duckworth, 1991.
Sambursky, S., 'On the possible and probable in Ancient Greece', *Osiris*, 12 (1956), 35–48.
Sandberg, A. and Bostrom, N., *Global Catastrophic Risks Survey, Technical Report #2008-1*, Future of Humanity Institute, Oxford University, 2008.

Sarris, P., 'Climate and disease', in E. Hermans (ed.), *A Companion to the Global Early Middle Ages*, Leeds: Arc Humanities Press, 2020, pp. 511–38.
   'New approaches to the plague of Justinian', *Past and Present*, 254 (2022), 315–46.
Savage, S. L., *The Flaw of Averages: Why We Underestimate Risk in the Face of Uncertainty*, Hoboken, NJ: John Wiley, 2009.
Scheid, J., *An Introduction to Roman Religion*, trans. J. Lloyd, Edinburgh: Edinburgh University Press, 2003.
Scheidel, W., *Death on the Nile: Disease and the Demography of Roman Egypt*, Mnemosyne Supplements, Leiden: Brill, 2001.
   The Great Leveler: Violence and the History of Inequality from the Stone Age to the Twenty-First Century, Princeton, NJ: Princeton University Press, 2017.
   'Libitina's bitter gains: seasonal mortality and endemic disease in the ancient city of Rome', *Ancient Society*, 25 (1994), 151–75.
Schulz, F., *Classical Roman Law*, Oxford: Clarendon, 1951.
Sessa, K., 'The new environmental Fall of Rome: a methodological consideration', *Journal of Late Antiquity*, 12 (2019), 211–55.
Shaw, B. D., 'Did the Romans have a future?', *Journal of Roman Studies*, 109 (2019), 1–26.
   'Our daily bread', *Social History of Medicine*, 2 (1989), 205–13.
Sheynin, O. B., 'On the prehistory of the theory of probability', *Archive for History of Exact Sciences*, 12 (1974), 97–141.
Silva, P. G. et al., 'Archaeoseismic record at the ancient Roman city of Baelo Claudia (Cádiz, south Spain)', *Tectonophysics*, 408 (2005), 129–46.
Skinns, L., Scott, M. and Cox, T. (eds), *Risk*, Cambridge: Cambridge University Press, 2011.
Slovic, P., 'Perception of risk', *Science*, 236 (1987), 280–5.
Sonnabend, H., *Naturkatastrophen in der Antike: Wahrnehmung, Deutung, Management*, Stuttgart: J. B. Metzler, 1999.
Spiegelhalter, D., 'Quantifying uncertainty', in L. Skinns, M. Scott and T. Cox (eds), *Risk*, Cambridge: Cambridge University Press, 2011, pp. 17–33.
Sunstein, C. R., *Laws of Fear: Beyond the Precautionary Principle*, Cambridge: Cambridge University Press, 2005.
   Risk and Reason: Safety, Law, and the Environment, Cambridge: Cambridge University Press, 2002.
Taleb, N. N., *The Black Swan: The Impact of the Highly Improbable*, London: Allen Lane, 2007.
Taylor, R., *Roman Builders: A Study in Architectural Process*, Cambridge: Cambridge University Press, 2003.
Thompson, E. P., 'The moral economy of the English crowd in the eighteenth century', *Past & Present*, 50 (1971), 76–136.
Toner, J., 'Decadence in ancient Rome', in J. Desmarais and D. Weir (eds), *Decadence and Literature*, Cambridge: Cambridge University Press, 2019, pp. 15–29.
   Infamy: The Crimes of Ancient Rome, London: Profile, 2019.

'The intellectual life of the Roman non-elite', in L. Grig (ed.), *Popular Culture in the Ancient World*, Cambridge: Cambridge University Press, 2016, pp. 167–88.
Leisure and Ancient Rome, Cambridge: Polity, 1995.
Popular Culture in Ancient Rome, Cambridge: Polity, 2009.
Roman Disasters, Cambridge: Polity, 2013.
Treggiari, S., 'Lower class women in the Roman economy', *Florilegium*, 1 (1979), 65–86.
Tulloch, J., and Lupton, D., *Risk and Everyday Life*, London: Sage, 2003.
Versnel, H. S., *Coping with the Gods: Wayward Readings in Greek Theology*, Leiden: Brill, 2011.
Wallace-Hadrill, A., 'The senses in the market-place: the luxury market and eastern trade in imperial Rome', in J. Toner (ed.), *A Cultural History of the Senses in Antiquity*, London: Routledge, 2014, pp. 69–89.
Walsh, J. J., *The Great Fire of Rome: Life and Death in the Ancient City*, Baltimore, MD: Johns Hopkins University Press, 2019.
Watson, A., *The Spirit of Roman Law*, Athens, GA: University of Georgia Press, 1995.
White, R. J., *The Interpretation of Dreams = Oneirocritica by Artemidorus*, Park Ridge, NJ: Noyes Press, 1975.
Wildavsky, A., and Dake, K., 'Theories of risk perception: who fears what and why?', *Daedalus*, 119 (1990), 41–60.
Wilkinson, I., *Risk, Vulnerability and Everyday Life*, London: Routledge, 2008.
Wynne, B., 'May the sheep safely graze?', in S. Lash, B. Szerszinski and B. Wynne (eds), *Risk, Environment and Modernity*, London: Sage, 1996, pp. 44–83.
Yaron, R., 'Remarks on consensual sale (with special attention to periculum emptoris)', *Roman Legal Tradition*, 59 (2004), 59–76.
'Sale of wine', in D. Daube (ed.), *Studies in the Roman Law of Sale*, Oxford: Clarendon, 1959, pp. 71–7.
Zanda, E., *Fighting Hydra-Like Luxury: Sumptuary Regulation in the Roman Republic*, London: Bloomsbury Academic, 2013.
Zinn, J. O. (ed.), *Social Theories of Risk and Uncertainty: An Introduction*, Oxford: Blackwell, 2008.
Zola, I. K., 'Observations on gambling in a lower-class setting', *Social Problems*, 10 (1963), 353–61.
Zulaika, J., *Terranova: The Ethos and Luck of Deep-Sea Fishermen*, Philadelphia: Institute for the Study of Human Issues, 1981.

Index

accounting, 82–3
adultery laws, 119–21
Aesop, 100
amphitheatres, 63–8
annuities, 94–8
Antonine Plague, 108
Antoninus Pius, 108
anxiety, 100, 106, 107, 109, 111, 125–6
  and luxury, 115–19
apatheia, 108
apprentices, 36–7
architects, and liability, 75–7
architecture, 60–6
Armenia, 68
Arrian, 21
Artemidorus, 106–8
astrology, 34–5
Augustine, 21
Augustus, 22, 55, 64–6, 81, 119–21, 124
  and adultery laws, 119–21
  marriage laws, 81, 120
Aulus Gellius, 72–3

Baelo Claudia, 62
Beck, Ulrich, 1–3, 5, 12, 31, 36, 111–12, 125–7
begging, 39
black swans, 8
bottomry, 94
building techniques, 61–2, 63–4
buildings, collapse of, 25, 63–4
burial clubs, 98–9

Caligula, 64
Campus Martius, 64
Cannae, 117
Capital Asset Pricing Model, 7
casus fortuitus, 77–8
Cato the Elder, 88, 89–90
central banks, 12
chance, 47, 59. *See also* luck
charioteers, 51

childbirth, 105
children, 39–40
Christianity, 21, 114
Cicero, 16–17, 18–19, 20–1
civil law, 71
Claudius, 19, 42, 54, 94
climate change, 22–3
clothing supplies, 67
collateral, 92
collegia, 98–9
Colosseum, 62
Columella, 82–3
consensual sale, 78–9
contractors, 68–9
contracts, 71, 75–6
Corbulo, 68
Coronavirus pandemic, 1
Corpus Juris Civilis, 71
Crassus, 63
criminal law, 71
crop yields, 36–8, 83
curses, 45–6, 47, 106
cursus publicus, 69–70

danger, 9, 11, 76
deadhand control, 81–2
death, causes of, 29–30
debt, 103
debt cancellation, 86
default rates, 86–8
default risk, 85–6, 86–8
demography, 96, 99
depreciation, 83
dice, 19
dice oracles, 19–20, 57–8, 100–1
Digest, 71
Diocles, charioteer, 51–2
disasters, 25–6, 41, 113–14
diversification, 36–8, 47, 59, 88
divination, 17–18, 21, 44
donatives, 43–4

Dorotheus of Sidon, 34–5
Douglas, Mary, 10–11
dream interpretation, 106–8
drowning, 30

earthquakes, 25, 62–3, 76
edgework, 56
environmental risk, 65–6
Epictetus, 109
epitaphs, 29–30
Europe, Early Modern, 12
experts, 1–2, 114
exposure, 39–40

family, 103, 120
family management, 39–40
family planning, 39–40
famine, 37–8
fate, 2–3, 5, 7, 12, 15–19, 55
fideicommissa, 81–2
Fidenae, 63–4
financial management, 38–9, 82–99
fire, 26, 29, 64, 123. *See also* Great Fire of Rome
fishing, 79–80
flattery, 43–4
floods, 64–5, 76, 108
food shortage, 41–3
fortuna, 16–17, 47, 56–7. *See also* luck
Foucault, Michel, 11, 126–7
fraud, 69, 93
funerals, aristocratic, 50–1
future, conceptions of, 9–10, 11–12, 17–19, 20–2, 32, 113, 121, 127–9
  and law, 75–80
  and liability, 75–80
  ownership, 79–82
  and risk, 6–7, 10

Gaius, jurist, 71
gambling, 19, 53–6, 122
games, 119
Giddens, Anthony, 2–3, 12, 22
gladiators, 51, 58
gods, 16–19, 19–20, 44–7, 56–8
gossip, 41
graffiti, 41
Great Financial Crisis, 7
Great Fire of Rome, 3, 4, 26, 123, 128

hazards, 8–9
health, 35, 46
hiring, 78
history, 21–2

identity, 56–9, 108–9
incertae personae, 81
income risk, 83
infamia, 52, 81
inflation risk, 83
inheritance, 71, 80–2, 94–5
insulae, 63
insurance, 12, 93–4
interest rates, 83–9
intuition, 104
investment risk, 83

judges, 72–4, 80
Julius Caesar, 50, 52, 64, 109
Justinian, 71
Juvenal, 116

knucklebones, 16, 19–20

land, 82
law, 70–82, 105, 128
  and adultery, 119–21
  and moral risk, 116–19
  and probability, 72–5
  and uncertainty, 71–2
laws, sumptuary, 116–19, 126
legal risk, 86
lending, 82, 83–9, 103
letting, 78
Lex Falcidia, 80–1, 95
liability, 75–80
life expectancy, 23, 95–7
'limited good' hypothesis, 41, 50
Livy, 121
logistics, 19, 66–70, 128
luck, 16–17, 47–50, 55
luxury, 115–19

magic, 45–6, 47, 106
Marcus Aurelius, 22, 44, 108–9
maritime loans, 89–94
maritime trade, 50, 52–3, 79
market risk, 84–5
marriage, 103, 120
medicine, 27, 46, 105
mental health, 27
Mercury, 100
militarism, 115
military infrastructure, 128
mining, 77
morality, 111–24
morbidity, 26–7
mortality, 80, 97–8, 99, 102–3
mutualism, 40–1

Nero, 3, 128
nuclear war, 1, 3, 22–5, 31
numeracy, 53

oculus, 61
official posts, 104–5
oracles, 34–5, 45
Oracles of Astrampsychus, 35, 101–6
Ovid, 120

Pantheon, 61
Pascal, Blaise, 5–6, 10, 19
patronage, 43–4
Paulus, jurist, 71
pax deorum, 113–14
peasants, 36–7
periculum, 76, 77–8, 85
periculum emptoris, 78–9
persecution, 113–14
placebo, 47
plague, 24–5
Pliny the Younger, 123
Plutarch, 20
poison, 103, 105–6
Polybius, 21
Pompeii, 42, 63
poverty, 35, 38–40
pragmatism, 34–6
probabilistic thinking, 104
probability, 5–6, 7–8, 19–20
prodigies, 44
property, 71, 75–6
proverbs, 35–6

reciprocity, 40–1
relative risk, 83
religion, 44–7, 65, 99–108
  and risk, 113–14
religious innovation, 104
rental property, 82
requisitions, 68
reserves, 67
resilience, 108–9
riots, 42–3
risk, 1–14
  and antiquity, 3–5, 13–14, 15–31
  and anxiety, 125–6
  and blame, 126–7
  and culture, 10–12, 32–59
  definition, 6–10
  early use of term, 6
  environmental, 65–6
  etymology, 6
  and finance, 7–8
  and the future, 6–7, 10
  and identity, 56–9, 108–9
  and imagination, 30–1
  and law, 128
  and lay people, 33–4
  and luxury, 115–19
  and morality, 10–11, 111–24
  and politics, 10–11
  and religion, 113–14
  and social status, 28, 31
  and tradition, 32–5, 59, 121
  and volatility, 7, 100
risk aversion, 100
risk avoidance, 50, 53
Risk Culture, 32–4
risk discourse, 31, 112–13, 122–3, 125–7
risk management, 60–110
risk premium, 86–8
risk reduction, 92
risk and reward, 91–2, 93
Risk Society, 1–3, 33, 126–7. *See also* Beck, Ulrich
risk taking, 50–3
risk transfer, 90–1
rumour, 123
Rumsfeld, Donald, 8

sailors, 89
satire, 116
scapegoating, 114
Scipio the Younger, 115
sea travel, 49, 58–9, 79, 89, 92
self-sufficiency, 68
senate, 68
shipwreck, 26, 92
Sibylline books, 44, 65
slavery, 39
slaves, 72, 102
social relations, 40–1
social status, 41–4
societas, 88
sport, 50
Stoicism, 108–9
sumptuary laws, 116–19, 126
superstition, 44–5, 49
supply lines, 67–8
systemic risk, 88

taverns, 118, 122
tax, 67, 84, 86
Temple of Jupiter at Baalbek, 62
theft, 74–5
Theodosian Code, 71
Tiber, 64–6
Tiberius, 64
trade, 38, 82, 89–94, 115
transport, 67

travel, 26, 35, 103
treaties, 68
Trimalchio, 52–3, 89
trusts. See *fideicommissa*
Twelve Tables, 70
Tyche. See *fortuna*

Ulpian, jurist, 71
Ulpian's Table, 94–8, 128
uncertainty, 1–14, 15–22
urban administration, 66
usufructs, 80–1, 96
usury, 85

vestal virgins, 113
vigiles, 64
vines, 82–3

violence, 29–30
vis maior, 77–8, 79
vitium, 77–8
votive offerings, 46–7
vulnerability, 25–30
   and epitaphs, 29–30
   and gender, 27–8
   and social status, 28

water damage, 76–7. *See also* floods
wills, 80–2
wine, 79
witnesses, 72–3
women, 27–8, 35, 39, 40, 52, 118

Xenocrates, 20